# DEAN CLOSE SCHOOL

## LIBRARY

VERBUM DEI LUCERNA

This book must be returned by the latest date stamped below.

**Hampstead Heath.** A view of Hampstead Heath, in the background Ken Wood House by Robert Adam (no. 58).

# ARCHITECT'S
## GUIDE
### TO
# LONDON

## RENZO
## SALVADORI

Butterworth Architecture

London     Boston     Singapore     Sydney     Toronto     Wellington

First published in Great Britain in 1990
by Butterworth Architecture
an imprint of Butterworth Scientific

 PART OF REED INTERNATIONAL P.L.C.

Translated by Brenda Balich

© Renzo Salvadori, Canal Libri, Venice
ISBN 0 408 50056 5

Printed in Italy
Stamperia di Venezia, Venice
335-90

# Contents

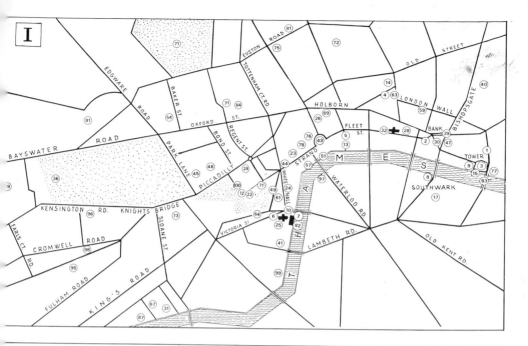

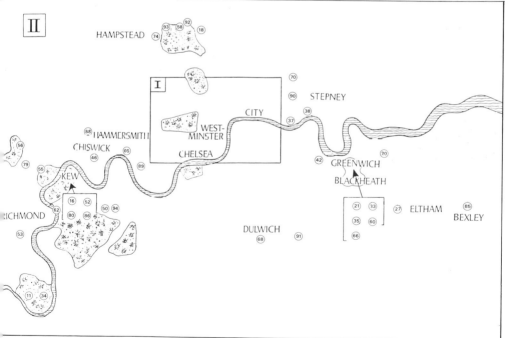

London maps. Figures refer to item numbers.

**Regent's Park.** Cumberland Terrace by John Nash (no. 71).

# FOREWORD

Butterworth Architecture intend this series of Architect's Guides to provide architects (and all those primarily interested in architecture) with a compact historical summary and description of over a hundred buildings in each city selected. The guides accordingly cover the fullest possible historical range, but unlike tourist guides describe buildings in full depth of architectural detail, as well as including a comprehensive section, in every case, on twentieth century architecture up to the present day. In addition every guide contains a description of a key design element characteristic of each city, not so much a building as a metaphor for that city. For London, the author found the great range of traditional shop signs exemplary.

In the late twentieth century urban planning and design has become a subject of key importance to all cities, and each city demonstrates its own historic solutions, as well as their related problems and the way in which these are being solved. A city is not only a collection of buildings: it has its own special environment, often more precious and fragile than the individual buildings which created it.

The urban development of London is dealt with here in some detail in view of its unique development as a collection of towns and villages that have gradually come together to form a variegated yet cohesive whole under the seemingly overwhelming pressures first of the industrial revolution in the eighteenth and nineteenth centuries and secondly through the growth of twentieth-century communications and technology.

This volume being nonetheless a particular selection reflects the personal taste, and prejudices too of the author. In the text this is balanced, and enhanced perhaps, by some of the best known authorities on English architecture, such as the late Sir Nikolaus Pevsner, Sir John Summerson, Sir James Richards, Henry Russell Hitchcock, and the late Ian Nairn, and others to whose works the reader may further refer (see Bibliography).

Finally, since we are dealing with a book in which the illustrations must play a primary role, both author and publisher wish to express their thanks to all those, photographers and librarians, who have given their co-operation. Their gratitude first of all to Romano Cagnoni and Frank Monaco, who dedicated so much time and energy as professional photographers. Thanks also to the librarians of the main photographic collections in London, and to the staff of the National Building Record and of the former Greater London Council. Staff of the British Travel Association were also of considerable assistance in the detailed preparation of the material.

**Mereworth, Kent.** The Villa Rotonda reproduced by Colin Campbell in 1723, one of the earliest buildings in the neo-Palladian
style.

every city is a living show, and the character of the show lies first of all in its scenic nature, produced by the density, as well as the quality, of the buildings and the urban space they create. In this sense London can be said to be disappointing; it is not as spectacular, at least not as immediately spectacular, as Paris, Rome or Venice. Nonetheless, London has the right to be called an architectural capital as few other cities have. Most of the principal builders in the history of English architecture have worked a great deal in London, so that London's buildings form an extraordinary complete anthology of the architecture of the country of almost all periods. What London lacks is certainly not quality, but density; London is, in fact, the most typical example of the «scattered» city, according to the definition given by Steen Rasmussen, in contrast with the «concentrated» city; it is the prototype of the polycentric, sprawling city; London, in a way, might be described as hardly a city at all, at least in the traditional Classical-Baroque meaning of the term, but as a collection of villages.

London is the city of separate communities, where architecture has to be discovered a little at a time. The fact that several of its boroughs, such as Chelsea, Hammersmith, Hampstead, Greenwich, etc., had different origins as independent country villages, gives a pleasant human scale to its urban environments; they already embody that ideal of «rus in urbe» that English architects tried consciously to follow when the principles of picturesque planning were first defined at the end of the XVIII century. The Inns of Court, the «greens» of Highgate and Richmond, the malls of Hammersmith, Chiswick and Twickenham, to mention a few examples, are extraordinarily picturesque and rural, though completely enclosed within the city. Important individual buildings, as well, such as Westminster Abbey, Greenwich Hospital or the Nash Terraces, which in other cities would have been outstanding elements of the urban scene, have been conceived surrounded and isolated by green, open spaces. London, for a number of reasons both historical and geographical, never enlarged the walls of the ancient Roman city, as did, for instance, Paris, but developed freely beyond them. London, moreover, was born bicephalous: the City, centre of commerce, on one hand, Westminster, royal citadel, on the other. This characteristic can be said to originate in Roman times. «That which the Romans created – writes Rasmussen in 'London, The Unique City' – and which was of vital importance for the history of London, is the great centre of communication, and it was that which determined the site of the city, for the importance of London – then as always – was primarily due to its position as the great centre of commercial policy. The city was not the seat of government. There were five towns which could be thus designated, but London was not one of them. The nearest was Verulamium, where St. Albans now lies, about 20 miles north of the

**St. Albans Cathedral.** One of the most imposing Norman churches in England, built in 1077-88 reusing Roman tiles and bricks from Verulamium.

**Canterbury Cathedral.** The eastern end, designed in 1174-84 by William of Sens, a Frenchman, is one of the earliest Gothic buildings in England.

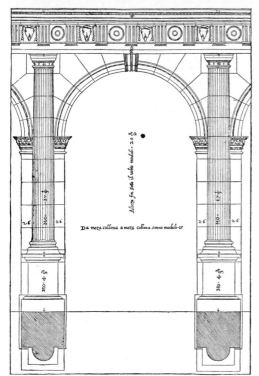

**The classical arch.** A plate from the «Quattro Libri dell'Architettura» (1570) by Andrea Palladio illustrating the Doric order. The Palladian influence on British architecture dates back to Inigo Jones (nos. 21-26) at the beginning of the 17th century.

**A London doorway.** A drawing by Peter Wyld from «London: The Art of Georgian Building» illustrating a doorway in Stoke Newington Church Street, London N 16: a very rich doorcase dating from the 1730s which shows both Palladian and Baroque (Gibbs) elements.

Thames. Possibly London originally was merely its port».

The six great Roman roads (1/b) that radiated from London can still be recognised today in Edgware Road (Watling Street towards St. Albans and Chester), for instance, Kingsland Road (Ermine Street towards Lincoln and York), Shooters Hill (Watling Street, again, towards Dover) etc. Already in Roman times the Westminster area was an independent settlement, or at least an important crossing point because the Thames there was particularly easy to ford.

Westminster's strategic importance was confirmed by the fact that a Benedictine community which was to become extremely influential in English medieval history, settled here in the VIII century. It was patronised by English kings before the Conquest and was later to attract the royal residence. The City, on the other hand, always preserved its independence; William the Conqueror never forced his hand here; he built, indeed, the Tower (3) in the South-East corner of the City walls, but he excluded it from the Domesday record of 1086; thus the special political position of the City was recognised since the beginning of its history.

Between the two centres of the City and Westminster, conveniently linked by the Thames, for centuries the principal route of communication in London, a number of mansions and convents were built, among them the Temple of the Knights Templars which was to become the seat of the Inns of Court. The Templars, an extremely wealthy order, erected one of the earliest examples of Gothic architecture in England (5), soon after the Choir of Canterbury was begun. It should also be noted here, that the City, which never became a political capital, was never a religious capital either; that privilege traditionally belonged to Canterbury.

Up to the beginning of the XVI century, London remained within the limits of the Roman walls, then came the population explosion of the Elizabethan age. In 1530, London had 50,000 inhabitants (that is to say only about 10,000 more than in Roman times), by 1605 its population had gone up to 255,000; but the number of people living within the walls was only about 75,000.

Therefore already in the late XVI century London was a «scattered» city, extending from the dock area of the East End (Poplar, Blackwall, Deptford) to Westminster. By then the Strand was completely built-up and the urban development reached the Lincoln's Inn, Covent Garden and St. Martin's Lane areas. The great vitality of XVI century England, the age of the Tudor Renaissance, is clearly visible in the architecture of the period while it began to assimilate the first classical elements, it developed in the most original manner the late Gothic style both in its religious buildings (10) and in the great stately houses of the Elizabethan and Jacobean age.

The great expansion of London continued throughout the XVII century; in 1660 its population reached the half million mark, and by the end of the century it was already up to 700,000, though in the meantime the city was struck by

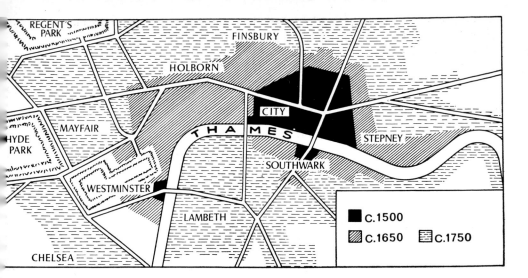

**C.1500** ■
**C.1650** ▨
**C.1750** ▥

**The growth of London.** From the beginning of the XVII century, London is already a «scattered» city, extending from the dock area of the East End to Westminster.

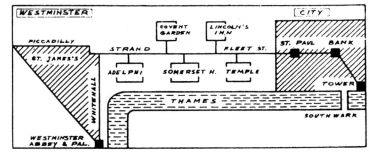

| WESTMINSTER | | | CITY |

PICCADILLY — ST. JAMES'S — STRAND — COVENT GARDEN — LINCOLN'S INN — FLEET ST. — ST. PAUL — BANK — ADELPHI — SOMERSET H. — TEMPLE — WHITEHALL — THAMES — TOWER — SOUTHWARK — WESTMINSTER ABBEY & PAL.

**The Two Cities.** A diagram showing the relation between the City of London and Westminster.

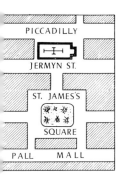

PICCADILLY
JERMYN ST.
ST. JAMES'S
SQUARE
PALL   MALL

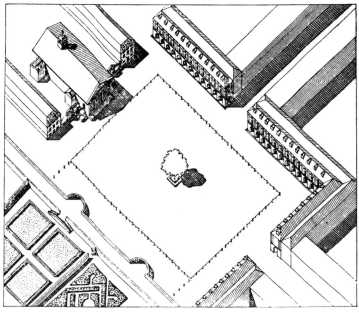

**17th century squares.** Covent Garden (no. 23) by Inigo Jones, a drawing from S.E. Rasmussen's «Towns and Buildings», right, and, above, St. James's Square, one of the best preserved London squares, its plan dates back to 1662 (see no. 29).

**Medieval London.** London Bridge, the only one to cross the Thames up to 1739, in a view by Wenceslaus Hollar of 1647, a few years before the Great Fire.

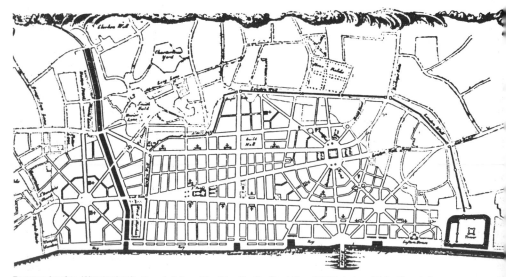

**Baroque London.** Wren's plan for the rebuilding of the City after the Great Fire of 1666, designed in the French Baroque manner.

wo terrible calamities, the plague of 1665, which illed 100,000 people, and the Great Fire of 1666. he Great Fire introduced a revolution in building echnique; instead of the timber-framed houses 5), easily destroyed by fire, new laws enforced he use of bricks. Bricks as building material vere indeed perfectly suitable to the new classi-al manner made fashionable by the architects f the Restoration, influenced by the Dutch tradi-on (27). Before starting work on the rebuilding f the City after the Great Fire, Wren proposed a lan for the whole area within the walls which vas based on wide, straight streets hinged on a umber of «rond points» in the French Baroque style, but the plan was not accepted. The City vas rebuilt following the old medieval pattern vhich is still recognizable today in the layout of nany streets.

3ut if the government never succeeded in regu-ating the development of London, a certain or-der was introduced, strangely enough, by private peculators, beginning from the late XVII century. he square and the streets with their rows of uni-orm terrace houses are certainly among the nost typical elements of London's townscape. he first square in London, Covent Garden, was designed by Inigo Jones in 1631 (23), then oth-ers followed, St. James's Square in 1663, 3loomsbury Square, Soho Square, etc. During he XVIII century the Mayfair and St. Marylebone areas were developed with Grosvenor Square, 3erkeley Square, Portman Square, etc., and dur-ng the first decades of the XIX century, it was the urn of Belgravia (72), Bloomsbury (75), Padding-on, Finsbury (73), etc. The principles for all these schemes remained practically unchanged, they nave been clearly pointed out by John Summer-son in his «Georgian London» as follows: «First: he principle of an aristocratic lead - the pres-ence of the landowner's own house in his square. Second: the principle of a complete unit of development, comprising square, secondary streets, market and, perhaps, church. Third: the principle of the speculative builder, operating as a middle-man and building the houses».

This system was able to be adopted with such success also because in the meantime the build-ng trade developed an almost standardised echnique for the mass production of houses. The architectural taste of the period, based on simplified classical-Palladian rules, was easily adaptable to these new building techniques. In-eriors, on the other hand, were often finished in he most lavish Baroque or Rococo style (48 and 54). Thus the coexistence of a number of factors ypical of XVIII century English society – the sys-em of land ownership, the renewal of building echniques, architectural taste and economic and demographic expansion – gave London, and other cities in Britain, like Bath or Edinburgh, their characteristic aspect, ordered and, at the same time, spacious; rational though easily adaptable to subtle variations of style and plan-ning. Classical London is therefore more the pro-duct of the speculative builder than of public planning; this can also explain the absence, al-ready noticed, of that monumental character that

Continental capitals clearly have in their city centres. But that does not mean that London ar-chitects did not produce private developments of considerable significance and size; for example those by the Adam brothers which are the ear-liest and the most important before those of Nash, particularly the Adelphi (57), Portland Place and Fitzroy Square.

During the XVIII century the population of London had a rather limited growth, passing from 750,000 at the beginning of the century to the 859,000 of 1801. London went through a second and more dramatic population explosion during the XIX century, by 1901 it reached 4,425,000 in-habitants, contained within the area of the former London County, from Woolwich to Hammer-smith, from Hampstead to Streatham. The first underground railway, the Metropolitan Railway, was opened in 1863, a revolutionary technique in the field of public transport introduced in an ef-fort to overcome the drawbacks inherent in the extraordinary expansion of the city.

Scattered city, city and country, the country in the city, the garden-city; another typical product of English taste which was to have considerable influence both in Europe and America and which can be traced back to the classical, aristocratic culture of XVIII century England. At this point we should perhaps outline briefly the development of one of the most original contributions of En-glish taste to European culture, the landscaped garden. The landscaped garden originated as a reaction to the geometrical Baroque garden in the French tradition, at the time when the Pallad-ian style became fashionable in architecture (46). The Palladian style itself was patronised by the «Whig» aristocracy as a symbol of indepen-dence in relation to the Baroque tradition remi-niscent of the absolutist tendencies of the former Stuart dynasty. The rigorously geometrical inter-pretation of certain Palladian buildings, such as the Villa Rotonda, faithfully reproduced more than once by English XVIII century architects, and first of all by Colin Campbell, at Mereworth, in 1723, can be seen as an anticipation of the neo-classical taste which was to rule European archi-tecture from the middle of the XVIII century on-wards. Classicism in architecture was in fact the counterpart of philosophical rationalism; and since for the philosopher of that period reason and nature were synonymous, we may thus ex-plain the apparently contradictory combination of classical Palladian architecture with the infor-mality of the English garden.

On the other hand, it must be borne in mind that the classical portico of the house just as much as the Greek temple in the garden were in fact ro-mantic, idealised interpretations of classical an-tiquity; architecture is seen here as an ornament of the landscape, as it was in the paintings of Claude Lorrain. If the landscaped garden has its beginnings with William Kent (46), it reached its most spactacular and complex development to-wards the middle of the century, as at Stourhead, for instance, where an amateur designer, Henry Hoare, about 1740, dammed a river to create a vast artificial lake, planted the surrounding bare

hills with a great variety of trees and bui
temples, bridges and grottoes; thus anticipatin
by a decade the style of the most celebrate
master of English gardening, «Capability» Brown
This love for nature and life in the open air, so ty
pical of the English people, can be explained
first of all, by the fact that England enjoys an ex
ceptionally mild climate, without the seasona
excesses of continental regions. But it must also
be borne in mind that English civilisation is basi
cally the product of an aristocratic, feudal socie
ty, tied more to the country than to the city. The
principal residence of the great English lan
downing families was in fact the country house
which was often a palace in the grand manner
surrounded by a park in the middle of a vast es
tate. The house in the city was little more than a
«pied-à-terre».

It is not surprising therefore if the English wante
their cities to have somehow a countrified
aspect. John Wood the Younger was the first ar
chitect who successfully brought nature to the
city by inserting a green open space in front o
his Royal Crescent at Bath in 1767. The Pictures
que movement which developed at the end of the
century was then to introduce the principle o
landscaped gardening in the enclosed city
square; the first example in London being Rus
sell Square laid out by Humphry Repton in 1800
Following the same principle John Nash planned
the grand design of Regent's Park-Regen
Street, in particular, the garden-suburb of Park
Village West (71). More ambitious, and certainly
more influential was to be the garden-suburb o
Bedford Park, begun by Norman Shaw in 1875
and formed by detached, semi-detached and
terrace houses which vary in style from late
Gothic to Queen Anne. These types of houses
were to be repeated countless times in the end
less, monotonous extensions of suburban Lon
don.

Even more depressing was the development o
the poor areas in the East End. England, having
started the Industrial Revolution, had to face the
problem of urban expansion on unprecedented
scale before any other European country had
done so. In order to find a radical solution to this
grave social problem, which meant unhealthy
houses and an enormous waste of time to cove
the great distances to and from the place of work
for the majority of the city dwellers, an English re
former, Ebenezer Howard, first had the idea o
the garden-city, which was clearly expressed in
his book «Tomorrow, a Peaceful Path to Real Re
form», of 1898. The garden-city, according to
Howard, was to combine the advantages of the
city with those of the country, excluding the
drawbacks of both; it had to be an autonomous
urban centre, an agreeable place to live but also
to work, with a clearly defined industrial area
The first garden-city realised according to Ho
ward's principles was Letchworth, in Hertford
shire, a few miles North of London, planned by
Barry Parker and Raymond Unwin in 1903; a se
cond example was Welwyn Garden City, again in
Hertfordshire, built by Louis de Soissons and
A.W. Kenyon about 1920. The same architects o

**The terraced house.** Axonometric of a pair of typical Georgian terraced houses. This illustration and those of the following page are from Peter Wyld's book «London: The Art of Georgian Building» (London, 1975), an excellent study both as regards the text and particularly the illustrations, which gives a splendid account of a period when «never had standards of taste and execution stood higher» (Summerson).

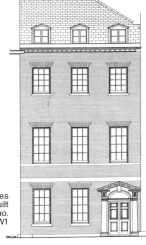

**London houses.** Left, houses in Denmark street, WC2 (built about 1680); right, house at no. 43 Parliament Street, W1 (1753).

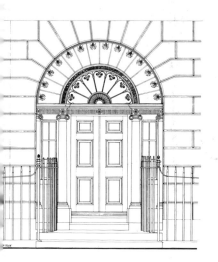

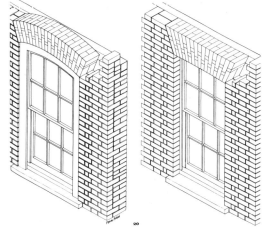

**Georgian buildings.** From the late seventeenth century until the early nineteenth century, London houses were built with almost standardised systems, bound by strict regulations which, however, allowed for subtle formal variations which mark the periods and the hand of the different architects.

The street doors are most characteristic: above left, an elegant entrance at no. 7, Mansfield Street, W1, dating from the late eighteenth century, in the Adam style. Above right, door dating from 1790 in Huntley Street, WC1.

In 1709, a Building Act prohibiting wooden window frames from being flush with the outside walls was passed – a safety measure against fires; the drawings (right) illustrate the change. Drawings by Peter Wyld from «London: The Art of Georgian Building».

20

**An 18th century square.** Bedford Square, Holborn, is a typical 18th century square, preserved completely on all sides, built perhaps b
Thomas Leverton, begun 1775.

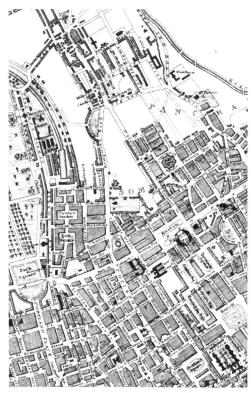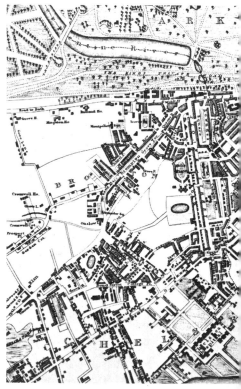

**Early 19th century London.** At the end of the Georgian period, early 19th century London was still surrounded, to a great extent, by open country, as the map reproduced here clearly shows: above left, the area N of Bloomsbury and St. Pancras (E of Regent's Park) and, above right, the area S of Hyde Park, Westminster.

etchworth, Parker and Unwin, also designed Hampstead Garden Suburb in 1906.

These centres, which underwent a certain though limited expansion, remained isolated examples. The idea of the garden-city, or, better, of the new town, became part of the national policy with the first Labour government after the war, following the proposals of the «Plan for the London Region» by Sir Patrick Abercrombie of 1944. Around London, beyond the «green belt», there are now eight new towns, Basildon, Bracknell, Crawley, Harlow, Hatfield, Hemel Hempstead, Stevenage and Welwyn, with a total population which will finally reach half a million.

The new towns, fifteen in all in Britain, including the eight satellites of London, established by the New Towns Act of 1946, have perhaps the defect of being too much of the garden-city type, that is, lacking in urban character, excluding Cumberauld in Scotland, one of the best also from the architectural point of the view. But it is certain anyway that «the English Picturesque theory – if not the practice – has an extremely important message – as Nikolaus Pevsner says in his Englishness of English Art'. We are in need of a policy of healthy, attractive, acceptable urban planning». This message seems to have been well received and put into operation by a number of English planners and particularly by the London County Council which, since the war, rebuilt over a tenth of the area of the County. But what counts most is not only the quantity but the quality of the work done by the London County Council (carried on by the Greater London Council, formed in 1965), from both the architectural (94) and the town planning (95) point of view. Some of the most civilised characteritics of English architectural and planning tradions throughout the centuries seem to be continued in the new, vast London housing schemes, such as Roehampton. They should be examples of how to solve the problem of the city, that problem which is perhaps the most dramatic that contemporary civilisation in all countries has to face.

**Stourhead, Wiltshire.** Perhaps the most spectacular landscaped garden ever conceived, designed around 1740 by an amateur who completed it with ornamental temples, bridges and grottoes.

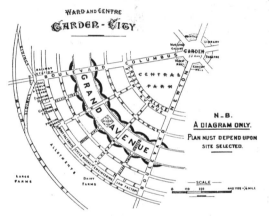

**The ideal city.** A ward of the garden-city designed by Ebenezer Howard. Notice the clear separation of the industrial area from residential districts.

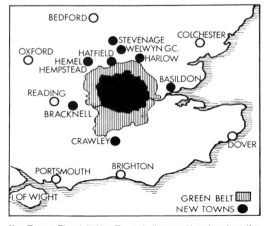

**New Towns.** The eight New Towns built around London since the war, beyond the «green belt».

# Bibliography

## General Works

H.R. Hitchcock, Architecture XIX and XX Centuries (The Pelican History of Art 1963). It includes one of the best accounts of Victorian architecture.

E. Kaufmann: Architecture in the Age of Reason (Hayward College 1955). A comparative analysis of Neo-Classical architecture in England, France and Italy.

G.E. Kidder Smith: The New Architecture of Europe (Pelican Books 1961). A selection of the best buildings in Europe since the war by a well-known American expert.

N. Pevsner: An Outline of European Architecture (Pelican Books 1953). An indispensable book.

N. Pevsner: The Englishness of English Art (Architectural Press 1956). An illuminating book on the principal characteristics of English art.

N. Pevsner: Pioneers of Modern Design (Pelican Books 1960). The origins of modern architecture and design from William Morris to Walter Gropius, by the best-known authority on the subject.

A. Powers: Shop Fronts (Chatto & Windus 1989). The evolution of the shop front from the 18$^{th}$ century, a unique account.

J.M. Richards: An Introduction to Modern Architecture (Penguin Books 1961). The development of modern architecture seen also in relation to building techniques and materials with special emphasis on the English contribution.

J.M. Richards: The Functional Tradition in Early Industrial Buildings (Architectural Press 1958). The most complete account of British industrial architecture, with a fascinating collection of pictures by Eric de Maré.

J. Summerson: Architecture in Britain 1530 to 1830 (The Pelican History of Art 1953). The standard work on the period.

## On London

B.R. Brown: An Art Guide to London (Ancho Books, New York 1952). A comprehensive list o the most significant buildings in London and sur rounding region.

D. Cruickshank & Peter Wyld: London, The Art o Georgian Building (The Architectural Pres 1975). A classic study, the finest illustrated ac count of the greatest period of British architec ture, the perfect companion to John Summer son's «Georgian London»; measured drawing splendidly executed by Peter Wyld.

W.H. Godfrey: A History of Architecture in anc around London (Phoenix House 1962). A boo that is exactly and comprehensibly what its title says.

I. Nairn: Nairn's London (Penguin Books 1965). A very personal and brilliant analysis of London' architecture and townscape.

N. Pevsner: The Buildings of England (Penguir Books 1952-57). A uniquely comprehensive sur vey of architecture in London and other countie: by an historian who is also a specialist on mo dern architecture.

S.E. Rasmussen: London the Unique City (Pen guin Books 1960). A complete account of the de velopment of London from Roman times.

J. Summerson: Georgian London (Pleiade: Books 1948). An invaluable book for the under standing of London.

London Transport Publications include a consi derable number of booklets and leaflets, ver inexpensive and often free (available from mos Underground booking offices), which provide ; surprisingly varied selection of practical and reli able guides to many aspects of London art anc life.

## ROMAN LONDON

During the entire period of Roman occupation in the British Isles (43 - 410 A.D.), London (Londinium) was the most important city in the country: principal river and sea port and the junction of a system of roads which radiated in all directions. Since that time the function of London has remained unchanged. The perimeter of the walls built in the second century still marks today the boundaries of the square mile of the City. With a population of about 40,000 inhabitants, London was one of the five largest cities of the Roman Empire North of the Alps. Built on two hills, Cornhill and that of St. Paul's on the banks of the Thames, it was bounded on the west by the River Fleet, and had Walbrook, a stream which has since disappeared, running through it. Almost on the exact site of London Bridge, a Roman bridge joined the city to the South bank, Southwark, and the roads leading to ports on the South coast. Cornhill was the first inhabited centre, and here was built the Forum, and the large basilica which stretched along the whole of its North side for a length of 420 ft. There are few remains of Roman buildings in London today: some parts of the city walls, fragments of buildings, mosaics and statues.

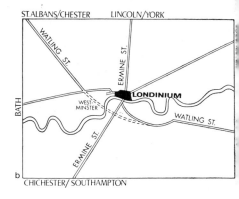

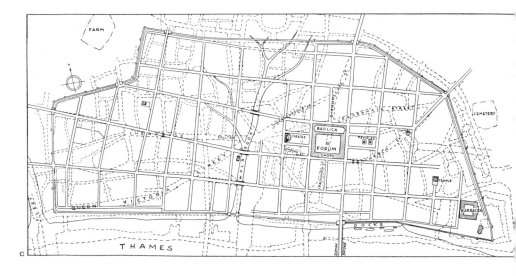

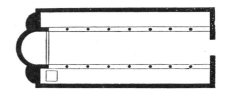

**ROMAN WALL, II c.** The Roman wall, erected at the end of the II c., was more than 2 miles long, seventy feet high and nine feet wide at its base. It was built on alternate layers of bricks and stone, surrounded by a moat; gates and forts (see White Tower) were spaced irregularly along its perimeter. Remains of this powerful defensive work can still be seen, though the upper part is mainly medieval. The illustrated section (1/a) shows, in the lower part, the classical, rational Roman building technique. [Trinity Place].

**2**

**TEMPLE OF MITHRAS, II c.** The Temple of Mithras, built in the II c. on the bank of the Walbrook, is one of the most important buildings found in Britain. Basilican in plan, with nave and aisles separated by columns, and an apse, it measures 60 x 20 ft. «Insisting upon a high standard of conduct in human relationships, Mithras was also much admired by business-men and traders ... the Walbrook temple, with its rich equipment of fine statues and the rest, provides the contrast with the more rugged military temples as the shrine of a wealthy commercial community» (Pevsner). [Queen Victoria Street].

## THE NORMAN HERITAGE

We know very little about the period from the retreat of the Roman troops (410) up to the Norman Conquest (1066): the period which saw the Saxon and the Viking invasions, and of which almost nothing remains. It could be said that the history of England and its architecture begins with William the Conqueror, duke of Normandy, who brought with him the French language and culture. He set up a new centralised system of government which was extraordinarily efficient, both in politics and in religion.

«The Norman style in architecture, the most consistent variety of the Romanesque style in the West, strongly influenced France during the eleventh century; in England it did more than that: it made English medieval architecture» (Pevsner) The first important church in this style, Westminster Abbey, preceded the Conquest; built by Edward the Confessor, little of it remains today The White Tower, on the other hand, remains intact; one of the most imposing and significan buildings erected by William the Conqueror soon after the building of a similar fortress a Windsor. The great churches of this period are however, all out of London: St. Albans, Ely, Durham, etc. In the capital some crypts are still extant (Westminster, St. Mary-le-Bow, St. John's together with the choir of St. Bartholomew-the Great, which bears witness to the remarkabl development of the Norman tradition on this side of the Channel.

3a

Chapel of St. John in the White Tower.

**3**

**4**

**WHITE TOWER, 1078-97.** The White Tower, built of stone especially imported from Caen in France, was begun under William the Conqueror (1078) to dominate the perimeter of the City walls; it was erected near the S.E. Roman bastion. This typical early Norman hall-keep has a square plan and walls 12 ft thick at the foot. Externally (windows remodelled in the XVIII c.) it shows flat buttresses and angle turrets and at the S.E. angle the projection of the chapel. The interior consists of three floors, each one with three rooms. On the second floor we find the splendid **Chapel of St. John** (a), one of the purest examples of Norman architecture in England. Tunnel-vaulted nave with gallery, the aisles form an ambulatory behind the altar. The bare walls and the unmoulded arches emphasize the clarity of this architecture which gives the impression of having been carved in the stone by the hand of a giant. [Tower of London].

**ST. BARTHOLOMEW-THE-GREAT, 1123.** Of the ancient church, founded as an Augustinian Priory in 1123 at the same time as the adjoining hospital, only the chancel and part of the crossing remain today. The chancel had an apsed end with ambulatory and three radiating chapels which have now disappeared. What remains still gives an impressive picture of the powerful Norman architecture of the period. The chancel has circular piers with finely moulded capitals and gallery of four arched openings with one relieving arch in each bay. Clerestory window replaced in the XIV c. The E. end of the gallery is XIX c. [West Smithfield].

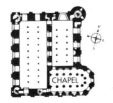

# GOTHIC ARCHITECTURE

This is the central period of the Middle Ages, from the end of the twelfth century to the end of the fifteenth century: the Hundred Years War (1337-1453) and the Wars of the Roses (1455-1485) proved to be the decisive elements in the formation of the nation.

At the end of the twelfth century when the Gothic style makes its appearance on this side of the Channel, England was, culturally, still a province of France (the French language was used officially until 1362). A Frenchman, Guillaume de Sens, was, in fact, the architect of the first Gothic building in England, the choir of Canterbury (1175). At roughly the same time, the Temple church was built, and, at the beginning of the thirteenth century, the choir of this church, Southwark Cathedral, and later, Westminster Abbey. It might be useful to remind readers of the traditional divisions of English Gothic: Early English (1180-1307), Decorated (1307-1377), and Perpendicular (1377-1509). To the first period belong the London buildings mentioned above; these, although inspired by the architecture beyond the Channel, do show some typically English characteristics: the Chapter Houses, for example, such as those of Westminster, Salisbury and Lincoln. With their large square windows, they already look forward to the so-called Perpendicular style of architecture. The hall, used as dining room and main living room of the large English houses ever since the medieval period, is another characteristic element in English architecture.

The portal of St. Bartholomew, XIII c., house of 1595 (no. 4).

St. Helen Bishopsgate, 14th-15th Century.

The portal of the Temple Church, 1160-85 (no. 5).

**TEMPLE CHURCH, 1160-1240.** This church of the Knights Templars dates from two different periods, the circular nave was built between 1160 and 1185, while the chancel was added in 1220-40. Both considerably restored in the XIX c. and after the war. It is one of the only four surviving examples in England of round churches, adopted by the Templars on the model of the Holy Sepulchre in Jerusalem. The Temple Church, erected during the transitional period between Norman and Gothic, shows the two styles side by side. The portal is Norman, while the porch in front has Gothic details; the round nave, surrounded by six Purbeck marble piers and rib-vaulted ambulatory, has pointed arcade arches in perfect Gothic style; the triforium above, instead, with blind arcades of intersecting arches, carries on the Norman tradition. On the floor Purbeck marble effigies of XIII c. knights. The chancel, begun in 1220, has aisles of the same height as the nave and «it is – as Pevsner says – one of the most perfectly and classically proportioned buildings of the XIII c. in England, airy, yet sturdy, generous in all its spacing, but disciplined and sharply pulled together». [The Temple].

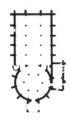

Plan of the Temple Church.

## 6

**WESTMINSTER ABBEY, XIII and XIV c.** Westminster Abbey is the most famous church in England not only for the beauty of its architecture but also for its intimate links with nine centuries of English history. The previous church had been erected by Edward the Confessor, the last Saxon king who was later canonized. In 1245, Henry III, one of the greatest patrons of art in the history of the country, decided to rebuild the abbey completely in honour of Edward the saint king, whose remains were placed in the chapel behind the great altar. The architect was Henry of Reims, a Frenchman, as appears from his name, who built it in the classical French Gothic style. Work progressed up to 1269, when the church was almost complete except for the last few bays towards

the main entrance where the previous Norman structure was left. The Abbey was completed, following the original XIII c. style, towards the end of the XIV c. by Henry Yvele, the architect of Westminster Hall. At the beginning of the XVI c. the Henry VII Chapel was added (10). The **West Front** (a), designed by Yvele, was also finished at the beginning of the XVI c. The towers are an XVIII c. work by N. Hawksmoor. The rest of the exterior was drastically restored in the XIX c. The interior is magnificent. The **nave** (c) is unique in England for its vertical thrust; it is in fact the highest of any English Gothic church, 102 ft. The chancel ends in five sides and is surrounded by an ambulatory with radiating chapels. The round piers of the nave are of Purbeck marble and at the four corn-

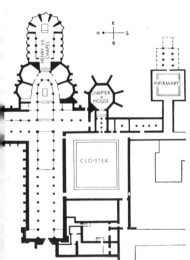

c

rs of the crossing they rise majestically to the eight of the vault. The gallery has two twin openings with a cinquefoil in a circle above for each ay, while the clerestory has a large twin window or each bay. The cloister was also built at the ame period as the Abbey and finished in the XIV . On the E side we find the beautiful **Chapter House** (g, h), again of the same period (1245-50) s the church. We cross a short outer vestibule which is followed by an inner vestibule with much igher ceiling and where a staircase ascends to the Chapter House, which is entered through a chly carved double doorway. The Chapter House is an extremely luminous octagonal hamber where the wide four-light windows (40 high and 20 ft wide) fill the whole wall space.

Original XIII c. tiles on the floor. The Abbey is extraordinarily rich in funerary monuments. The most ancient and the most precious is certainly the **shrine of Edward the Confessor** (d), a goal of pilgrimage throughout the Middle Ages. Its base is a typical Cosmati work by Peter of Rome of 1270. The same Italian artist designed also the pavement of the Chapel as well as that in front of the high altar. His last work in the Abbey is the **tomb of Henry III** (e), the bronze effigy of the king by William Torel (1291) is a masterpiece of English Gothic sculpture. To the second period of the Abbey dates the extremely ornate **tomb of Edward III** (f) who died in 1377, a characteristic work in the Decorated Gothic style.

d

e

f

g

**Funerary monuments in Westminster Abbey.** (d) Shrine of Edward the Confessor, 1270; (e) Tomb of Henry III, 1291; (f) Tomb of Edward III, 1377; (g) Tiles on the floor of the Chapter House, XIII c.

The Chapter House, XIII c.

## 7

**WESTMINSTER HALL, 1394-99.** This great hall is the most important remaining part of the old Palace of Westminster. Originally built in 1097, it was then the largest hall in Europe. Henry Yvele rebuilt it in 1394-1402 preserving the lower parts of the Norman wall and thus the original dimensions (240 ft long and 100 ft wide). Its hammer beam roof is probably the finest existing in Europe: «The continent has nothing to emulate these achievements of a ship-building nation (These roofs) are in fact strongly reminiscent of ship's keels upside down». (Pevsner)

View of Westminster Bridge, in the background Westminster Hall and Westminster Abbey, a drawing by Canaletto c. 1747 (British Museum).

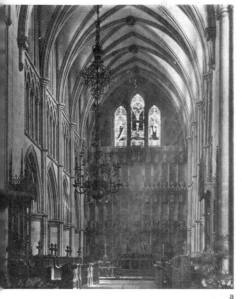

a

**OUTHWARK CATHEDRAL, XIII-XIV c.** Originally
e church of the old Augustinian Priory of St.
ary Overie (cathedral since 1905), it was rebuilt
 the beginning of the XIII c. Its present nave was
ompletely reconstructed in the XIX c.; only the
rossing, chancel and retrochoir, therefore, be-
ng to the ancient medieval church. Splendid
redos (1520), characteristic work of the Per-
endicular period (statuary modern). Edmund
hakespeare († 1607), William's brother, is bu-
ed here. We are only a few steps away from the
te of the «Globe».

## 9

**TOWER OF LONDON (BYWARD TOWER), XIII c.**
It was Henry III, the king of Westminster Abbey,
who began, in the second half of the XIII c., both
the inner and the outer walls of the Tower of London around the White Tower (4). In spite of addi-
tions and restorations the Tower of London still
remains today the most important work of military architecture in England. Of particular interest
is the Byward Tower (XIII c.) which preserves a
portcullis with its winch and an early XIV c. wall
painting.

b

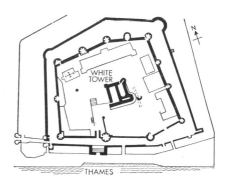

# THE TUDOR RENAISSANCE

During the sixteenth century, England began to assert herself for the first time on the international scene; it is also the time of the voyages of Drake and Raleigh. The philosopher Francis Bacon, the composers Orlando Gibbons and William Byrd and the poets Ben Johnson and John Donne and William Shakespeare, belong to this century.

While the first influences of the Classical Italian Renaissance can be felt, Perpendicular architecture underwent a change: arches are flattened, and there are huge windows everywhere, more glass than wall, it has been said. The decoration of ceilings is achieved by thickly ribbed vaults, elaborated so as to take on the characteristic fan form. The masterpieces of this period are the Royal chapels of Westminster, Windsor and Cambridge. The traditional division of English architecture into Perpendicular, Tudor and Jacobean ought not to be taken too strictly. In point of fact, late Gothic evolves slowly, being gradually influenced by Italian, Dutch and Flemish architecture. The secular buildings corresponding to the Royal chapels are the magnificent country houses of the second half of the century, Longleat, Wollaton Hall, Hardwick Hall, etc. It was in this still Gothic, and in many ways provincial, atmosphere that Inigo Jones served his apprenticeship as stage-designer before applying himself to architecture. The best known British painter of the period was Nicholas Hilliard; during the early part of the century the great German artist Hans Holbein the Younger worked at the court of Henry VIII.

Hans Holbein the Younger, Portrait of Henry VIII, 1540 (Ror. Galleria Nazionale).

Hardwick Hall, Derbyshire, 1590-97.

b

# 0

**CHAPEL OF HENRY VII, 1503-12.** Built probably by Robert Vertue between 1503 and 1512, where the Lady Chapel used to stand, it is one of the most splendid examples of Perpendicular Gothic style. Its **exterior** (b), although sumptuously decorated (bow-windows with complex broken plans, buttresses surmounted by niches, statues and domes with finials) still shows the sturdy and tenorous structure of the architecture of the period. Fantastic is the wealth of ornaments of its **interior** (a): in the nave, aisles and radiating chapels and particularly in the tracery of the fan vaulting. The tomb of Henry VII is the masterpiece of the Florentine sculptor Pietro Torrigiani (1512) and it is the earliest example of Italian Renaissance art in England. [Westminster Abbey].

c

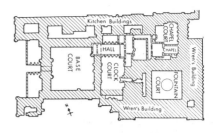

## 11

**HAMPTON COURT, 1515-20.** Hampton Court, built by Cardinal Wolsey, Henry VIII's counsellor, between 1515 and 1520, and one of the principal royal residences, is one of the most impressive Tudor buildings in England. The present palace is gathered around two courtyards (the third added by Wren in the XVII c. - see 34), each entered through tall gatehouses which show the medallions designed by Giovanni da Majano (1521), who was among the first Italian artists to work in Tudor London. On the N side of the Clock Court rise the impressive walls of the Great Hall, while the S side is taken by Wren's colonnade. This is the great age of brick: the tall chimney stacks which rise from the roof, each one with a separate shaft composed of brickwork of the most intricate patterns, become a spectacular decorative element of this architecture. But the most fascinating aspect of Hampton Court, as of all great Tudor buildings, is the wide expanses of the courtyards surrounded by solid, ferruginous wall masses.

## 2

**T. JAMES'S PALACE, XVI c.** This picturesque
ed-brick palace, built for Henry VIII towards the
iiddle of the XVI c., became the official royal re-
idence from 1698 (when Whitehall was des-
oyed by fire) until 1837. The most significant
art of the palace is the Gatehouse flanked by
olygonal turrets which closes the vista of St.
ames's Street. The rest of the building has been
econstructed in various periods. The painted
eiling of the Chapel Royal is an early Renais-
ance work. [St. James's Street].

## 13

**CHARTERHOUSE, XVI c.** Very little remains of
the Carthusian Priory of the XIV c. The present
Charterhouse represents a rare example of a
large XVI c. mansion as it became since the dis-
solution of the monastery in 1545. The buildings
are grouped informally around various courts in
a manner which is still medieval, reminding us
more of a country house than of a city mansion.
Its decorative elements, on the other hand, show
the mannerist elements then fashionable. The
most important building, facing the Master Court,
is certainly the **Great Hall** (second half of the XVI
c.) with a beautiful fireplace, screen and ceiling
of the same period. Chapel and Great Gallery are
also remarkable. [Charterhouse Square, Fins-
bury].

## 14

**MIDDLE TEMPLE HALL, c. 1570.** A perfectly preserved example of an Elizabethan hall: porch, screen passage, high windows, great oriel window to the south and lantern with opening on the roof for the central fireplace. The double hammerbeam roof is one of the most beautiful in existence. The sumptuously decorated wood screen is a typical product of the mannerist style which influenced so much English Renaissance architecture.

## 15

**QUEEN'S HOUSE, TOWER OF LONDON, c 1540.** The charming row of half-timbered houses in the S-W angle of the Tower gives us an idea of how London looked in the years before the Great Fire of 1666. Bricks and stone were rare material in S-E England and it is therefore no wonder that these houses, built mainly of timber, have been mostly destroyed by fire. The Staple Inn (1586) in Holborn is another important ensemble of Tudor domestic architecture though considerably restored.

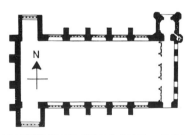

Plan of the Middle Temple Hall and, right, the wooden screen, 1575.

# CLASSICAL AND BAROQUE ARCHITECTURE IN THE SEVENTEENTH CENTURY

During the XVII c. the absolute powers of the king were dealt a mortal blow by the anti-monarchist Puritan revolution. Towards the end of the century, after 1688, England was on the way to becoming an almost constitutional monarchy, dominated by an oligarchy of the great aristocratic families.

During the early decades of the century, the so-called Jacobean period, architecture was still involving the styles of the previous century (late Gothic and Mannerism). During those years, Inigo Jones was creating his pure, classical buildings, but he was to remain an isolated case. The classical tradition was to be established later in England, only with the work of Wren in the second half of the century, strongly influenced by the Baroque style.

The first five buildings illustrated here represent the traditional English architecture of the first half of the century, that is, the buildings in which, in fact, both Inigo Jones and Shakespeare worked. They betray an England not yet sure of her use of the classical idiom, which had filtered from Holland and Flanders. The characteristics of this architecture (large square windows, unadorned symmetrical towers, bare walls and cubic structures) were, however, part of the typically English tradition which had matured during the previous century, and which were to persist throughout the evolution of later centuries.

## 16

**KEW PALACE, 1631.** Kew Palace, built in 1631 as a country house for a London merchant, known also as Dutch House, is one of the earliest examples of a style which originated in Holland and which was to become very popular in England. The classical ornaments, pilasters, columns, rustication, curved gables with crowning pediments, show an extremely refined brick technique and give this solid, middle-class building a restrained and civilised elegance. [Kew Gardens].

Typical Dutch houses of the XVI-XVII century, from S. Rasmussen's «Towns and Buildings».

## 17

**GEORGE INN, XVII c.** Though rebuilt in the second half of the XVII c., the George Inn, of which only one wing remains (the rest was demolished in 1889!), represents the sole surviving example in London of inns characteristic of Shakespeare's times. Early Elizabethan theatres, like the Fortune, had a square plan (later also with octagonal or circular plans) with wooden balconies all around similar to those of this inn. The George Inn, moreover, is close to the site where the Globe theatre used to stand. [Borough High Street, Southwark].

## 18

**CROMWELL HOUSE, 1637-40.** Another remarkable example of a red-brick house similar in style to Kew Palace: generous proportions and the minimum of decorations, heavy cornice and roof with dormer windows and cupola. The projection of the three centre bays and regularity of the five windows recall the design of Jones' Banqueting Hall. A splendid staircase inside, a masterpiece of the period. [Highgate].

## 19

**HOLLAND HOUSE, 1605-40.** This palace of the Earl of Holland, seriously damaged during the last war, represents the only example of a Jacobean house in central London. All that remains of this E-type plan building is the ground floor, with polygonal porch, the arched loggia running along the main block and the wings, and the E wing, with curved Dutch gables, all this considerably restored. The Gate Piers in the grounds are by Nicholas Stone based on designs by Inigo Jones (1629). [Holland Park].

## 20

**CHARLTON HOUSE, 1607-12.** An important and well-preserved Jacobean house, which shows very clearly the geometrical, angular purity of the architecture of the period: H plan, square turrets in the middle of the two wings, bay windows at the four ends of the wings, central hall which runs across the building from front to back. The only extravagant element is the W frontispiece, «the most exuberant and undisciplined ornament of all England» (Pevsner), which seems copied literally from one of the mannerist manuals then fashionable. [Charlton].

Plan of Charlton House.

**Inigo Jones** (1573-1652). He began his career as a painter, becoming stage-designer to the Court in the very same years in which Shakespeare was writing and producing his plays. He visited Italy twice, before 1603 and in 1613-14, when he made a thorough study both in Venice and Vicenza of the buildings of Palladio, and of the antique ruins in Rome. Appointed Surveyor of the King's Works in 1613, he was thus the first English architect to have a sound first-hand knowledge of both ancient and contemporary Italian architecture. A new era began for English architecture. The revolutionary importance of this architect can be measured by comparing those early buildings in the purest Palladian stye with the brick and half-timbered houses which made up the townscape of Jacobean London. Although he almost always took his inspiration from the work of Palladio, his style is extremely individual and is of a classical severity unknown at that time in Italy. As he wrote: «In architecture ye outward ornaments oft to be sollid, proporsionable according to the rulles, masculine and unaffected». He did however permit his interiors to be sumptuously decorated in the Baroque style, and justifying this, declared: «For as outwarly every wyse man carrieth a graviti in Publicke Places, whear ther is nothing els looked for, yet inwardly hath his immaginacy set on fire, and sumtimes licenciously flying out, as nature hir sealf doeth often tymes stravagantly, to delight, amase us sumtimes moufe us to laughter, sumtimes to contemplation and horror». And it is impossible to be more English than that.

a

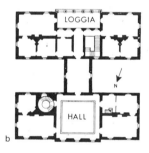

b

## 21

**QUEEN'S HOUSE, I. Jones, 1616-29.** Jones designed this house for Anne of Denmark, queen o' James I, in 1616; it is therefore the first fully classical building in the history of English architecture. Originally it was formed by two paralle blocks connected by a bridge across the Dover Road. When in 1662 the two sides were addec the house appeared as it is now with a square plan. The **south front** (a) overlooking the park, with loggia on the first floor, is a clear Palladian derivation (almost a Palazzo Chiericati in negative), while the **north front** (c) shows only a slight

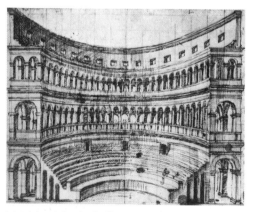

Inigo Jones, A drawing for the «masque» Albions Triumph, 1632 (Collection of the Duke of Devonshire).

projection in the central part which corresponds to the width of the hall, here a wide two-armed curved staircase gives access to the house. The hall, with a gallery around the upper floor, is a perfect cube (with a 40 ft side). The ceiling was once decorated by paintings of Orazio Gentileschi (1636), now in Marlborough House. The beautiful circular **Tulip staircase** (d), with no inner support, is inspired by the similar work designed by Palladio for the Convento della Carità in Venice. [Greenwich].

d

## 22

**QUEEN'S CHAPEL, I. Jones, 1623-7.** The first religious building in the classical style in England, erected as a Catholic chapel for the queen of the adjoining St. James's Palace. It is a plain parallelogram with pediments at both ends; on the W front it presents three windows, the central one arched. On the S side is the only surviving wing. The beautiful interior is also very simple, the most spectacular ornament being the wooden coffered vault. At the E end a large Venetian window, a type of opening here used for the first time and which was to become extremely popular with English architects. Most of the panelling dates from 1660-70. [Marlborough Road, Pall Mall].

## 23

**ST. PAUL COVENT GARDEN, I. Jones, 1631-8.** In 1631, Inigo Jones was commissioned to replan the area now occupied by the market and he laid out the first square in London (known also as the Piazza), following the model of Place des Vosges (1605) in Paris. On the N and E side he designed ranges of classical houses with tall arcades (all demolished in 1880-90!) and on the W side the present St. Paul's Church. This church, rebuilt to the original form after a fire in 1798, is characterized by the deep E portico, supported by square pillars at the angles and two Tuscan columns in the middle, and by the strongly projecting roof "powerful and affirmative in a way no later architect except Hawksmoor knew how to be" (Summerson).

a      b

c

**4**

**BANQUETING HALL, I. Jones, 1619-23.** Only remaining part of the ancient Whitehall Palace destroyed by fire in 1698. For the Banqueting Hall, designed three years after the Queen's House, Jones takes Palladio's architecture as a model once more, but he handles the various Palladian elements with a different spirit. «The façade, instead of converging to an emphatic centre, flows rhythmically from bay to bay, the slight projection of the three centre bays serving merely to give that fullness to the façade which so enhances the effect of mass ... he (Jones) was In search of a fiuality, a balance, more akin to the age of Bramante, and to this all his revisions of Palladio end. In this, too, he showed, all unconsciously, he phlegmatic Englishness of hls mind and its appropriateness as the source of the English tradition in classical design» (Summerson). The interior is formed by a **great hall** (b), with gallery all ound similar to that of the Queen's House, its size being based on the double cube 55x55x110 ft). The ceiling, subdivided in nine panels, incorporates the magnificent baroque **paintings by Rubens** (1630) representing the Apotheosis of James I (c). [Whitehall].

## 25

**ASHBURNHAM HOUSE, c. 1660.** A house built according to the most up-to-date taste of the period, it incorporates part of the wall of the previous XIV c. Prior's Lodging. The staircase is one of the masterpieces of the English Renaissance, its design is attributed to Jones himself or to his pupil John Webb. The architect has ingeniously exploited the limited space available, «...superb solution of a difficult problem...The spatial effect, especially the dramatic moment of finding oneself below the dome, must be experienced» (Pevsner). [Westminster School].

## 26

**LINDSEY HOUSE, I. Jones (?), 1640.** This hous built in 1640 is attributed to Inigo Jones or to on of his pupils (Stone or Webb). With its broad an solid proportions, giant Corinthian pilasters se parating the five windows, rusticated groun floor and crowning balustrade, it greatly in fluenced domestic architecture in England. Th adjoining house of 1730, which repeats the mo tifs of Lindsey House, bears witness to the conti nuing popularity of Palladian taste. [59/60 Lin coln's Inn Fields].

**27**

**ELTHAM LODGE, Hugh May, 1663-5.** The only surviving work by Hugh May (1622-84) whose style greatly influenced Wren and English domestic architecture as a whole. Built in 1663-5 or a London banker friend of Charles II, it derives directly from Dutch Palladianism (Mauritshuis, The Hague, 1633) which May knew very well. The house is of brick with large cornice at the eaves and hipped-roof, the central part of the main front has giant stone pilasters and pediments above. The interior, with a symmetrical plan, preserves a beautiful wooden staircase sumptuously decorated. A generation later (see 16 and 19), Holland still provides the architectural models which seem to suit the mercantile spirit of XVII c. England particularly well. [Court Road, Eltham].

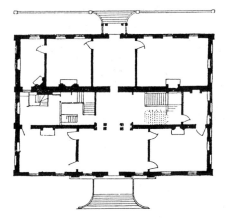

**Sir Christopher Wren** (1632-1723). Inigo Jones, as we have seen, was to remain an isolated case. For the real Classical Renaissance we have to wait for the fury of the Puritan revolution to pass. English architecture, and that of London in particular, was then dominated by the omnipresent figure of Wren. An astronomer who had become an architect, he retains something calculated and cold in his style which makes him waver between pure Classicism and real Baroque. He had been to Paris where he met Bernini, he made a thorough study of French architecture; Italian architecture too was not unknown to him. In 1666 the City of London was practically razed to the ground by the Great Fire. It fell to Wren to rebuild it, especially to reconstruct the many churches (52 in all), amongst them St. Paul's Cathedral, his masterpiece. He also designed three large palaces, Greenwich, Chelsea Hospital and Hampton Court, besides various buildings at Oxford and Cambridge. An ingenious, competent architect, who when he used the Baroque style, did so with great vigour and imagination (e.g. the steeple of St. Mary-le-Bow, his church towers in general, the interior of St. Stephen Walbrook, etc.) He tried perhaps to do too much and his amazing success as an architect was probably harmful to him. Faced with the mass of buildings by Wren, we cannot help wondering how many other architects failed to take the opportunities available. Certainly English architecture lost a great opportunity relegating an artist of the stature of Nicholas Hawksmoor to the function of draughtsman to Wren.

## 28

**ST. MARY-LE-BOW, C. Wren, 1670-83.** One o the most ancient London churches, the cryp preserves part of the Normal wall (1080-90). was rebuilt by Wren in 1670-83, it is therefor among his earliest works. Severely damage during the last war, the steeple, one of Wren' masterpieces, a superb Baroque invention, es caped miraculously intact. Above the bell-stage a balustrade and at the corners four large volute reach the airy rotunda of twelve columns; this i turn is crowned by a round balustrade wher other volutes support the top stage, a Gree cross aedicula, formed by twelve little columns then an obelisk with a 9 ft weather vane gryphor «London is the city of beautiful steeples», wrot Francesco Algarotti in 1753, and it still is, thank always to Wren. [Cheapside].

St. Paul's Cathedral, Choir Stall by Grinling Gibbons.

## 9

**T. JAMES'S, PICCADILLY, C. Wren, 1676-84.**
assical example of a Wren church with a longi-
dinal plan. According to the Protestant tradition
:veloped in Holland, the church did not need a
1oir or a transept, it was substantially a hall, of-
1 with galleries for extra seats, where the faith-
l gathered to hear the sermon. Built in connec-
1n with the development of the St. James's dis-
ct, it is, with St. Clement Danes, the only Wren
1urch outside the City boundary. Beautiful rere-
)s and font by Grinling Gibbons. [Piccadilly].

## 30

**ST. STEPHEN, WALBROOK, C. Wren, 1672-7.**
Modest exterior, if we exclude the ingenious
steeple. The interior, on the other hand, is one of
the most complex by Wren: a central-plan
church with dome, in a way a preparatory essay
for St. Paul's. The problem which Wren tried to
solve here is that of combining a church with
nave and aisles with a central space with dome.
From the entrance a series of columns directs
our attention towards the altar, the church «consists, we can read at once, in this W part, of a
nave with oblong groin-vaulted bays, aisles with
square flatceiling bays, and narrow outer aisles.
But almost at once it becomes clear that the
church is in fact not simply longitudinal, but
leads to a splendidly dominating dome with a
lantern to let light in from above. It is this ambigu-
ity between two interpretations of the space within what is really no more than a perfectly plain
parallelogram that connects St. Stephen with the
international Baroque, in spite of Wren's insis-
tence on the cool and isolated columns and on
classical decoration» (Pevsner). The dome, as in
St. Paul's, covers the width of the nave plus that
of the aisles, and it is supported by eight arches
and an equal number of columns. In spite of its limited size it is one of the most spacious and monumental of Wren's interiors. All furnishings are
original. [Walbrook].

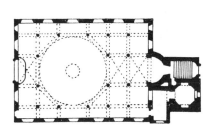

Plan of St. Stephen Walbrook.

## 31

**CHELSEA HOSPITAL, C. Wren, 1682-91.** This institution for veteran and invalid soldiers was founded by Charles II on the lines of the Hotel des Invalides (1670) in Paris. Wren's brick buildings are grouped round three open spacious courtyards, plain, almost homely, without any military pomp. A colonnade of slim tuscan columns runs along the main façade overlooking the river, the great portico with pediment, surmounted by lantern with dome, is the only decidedly Baroque element in the composition. To the left of the main vestibule there is the Hall and, to the right, the Chapel which has a Resurrection painted in the apse by Sebastiano Ricci (1710-15). See also no. 67.

## 32

**ST. PAUL'S CATHEDRAL, C. Wren, 1675-171**
The Seat of the Bishop and, with Westminst
Abbey, the largest church in London, St. Pau
Cathedral has very ancient origins, which g
back to the early Saxon period (604). The pre
ent fabric is the most important of Wren's work
begun in 1675. In this building Wren has su
cessfully assimilated, in a very personal wa
elements of different origins, both classical ar
Baroque. The front has, in the middle, a tw
storeyed portico of coupled columns with a ped
ment, flanked by two very Baroque towers whic
could have been inspired by Borromini. The ou
er walls of the nave show their direct origin fro
Inigo Jones's Banqueting Hall (24), though th
upper storey is only a screen to conceal the bu
tresses of the nave. The transept, with the sem
circular porches, go back again to Roman Bar
que (S. Maria della Pace). Finally the splend
dome supported by a colonnade all round th

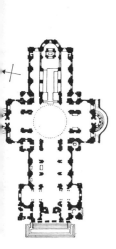

c

rum, recalls Bramante's project for St. Peter's.
his dome, almost a perfect hemisphere without
bs, crowned by a lantern is clearly a classical
vention in comparison with that of St. Peter's in
ome. Spacious and neatly composed interior,
gain classical in feeling, with Baroque orna-
ents. Nave with aisles, circular space under the
ome of the width of the nave plus that of the
isles (see 30). The chancel, with aisles, of three
ays, is of the same length as the nave, a longitu-
inal plan, therefore, more similar to a Norman or
othic church than to a Classical-Baroque one,
ut this was imposed on Wren. He had in fact
reviously designed a central-plan cathedral,
1e so-called Great Model, which was finally re-
cted by the clergy. The dome is decorated by
escoes, the Life of St. Paul, by James Thornhill
716-19). The choir stalls are the masterpiece
f Grinling Gibbons. Iron screens by Tijou.

d

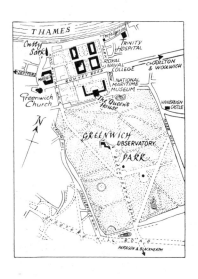

## 33

**GREENWICH HOSPITAL, C. Wren, 1696-1715.**
The Royal Naval College was originally a Naval
Hospital on the pattern of the Chelsea Hospital
for soldiers. The building was started as a Royal
Palace by John Webb (1663-9) who designed
the N-W block (to the right in the picture) in the
Renaissance style. Wren continued the project
taking Webb's façade as a starting point. Both
Vanbrugh and Hawksmoor co-operated with him
but the general plan is Wren's: the composition,
the most spectacular classical-Baroque complex in England, is based on two symmetric
groups of buildings with axis open towards th
Queen's House (21), «the space between them
more telling than the architecture itself, in spite
Wren's twin domes and colonnades. The inde
pendent life of space is of course a very Baroqu
conception» (Pevsner). The **ceiling of the Ha**
(see page 55), painted by James Thornh
(1707-17), is a masterpiece of English Baroqu
painting. (See also page 55 and no. 60).

c

**4**

**HAMPTON COURT, C. Wren, 1689-1702.** In 1689, Wren added to the old Tudor Palace of Hampton Court (11) the S-E wing, that is to say the E front towards the French garden, the **S front** (c) and the **Fountain Court** (b). It is one of the most French of Wren's buildings where the influence of Versailles is clear: low ground floor, main floor with tall windows and round windows above, attic with balustrade. The same scheme is applied to both fronts and in the Fountain Court. The gardens too are French in style, they were in fact designed by two pupils of Le Notre. In this palace again we find the work by the two crafts-men responsible for the most beautiful decora-tive elements in Wren's architecture, Grinling Gibbons and Jean Tijou. Tijou created the wrought-iron balustrade of the principal interior staircases, the twelve **Gates** (a) now in the Privy Garden and those in the Fountain Garden for Hampton Court. The virtuosity of this master of ironwork appears in all its magnificence in the central panels of these railings flanked by thin, plain vertical bars: a subtle counterpoint which gives extraordinary energy to this transparent masterpiece of baroque design.

d

**35**

**MORDEN COLLEGE, C. Wren (?), 1695.** A
almshouse for «decayed Turkey merchants», a
most certainly by Wren. Long, broad front wit
pediment and dome in the centre and sho
wings at the ends. The quadrangle, with lo
straight headed arcades of Tuscan columns an
pediments in the centre of each side, is domina
ed by the steep pitched roof which gathers a
around it, so that it gives us the impression of be
ing at the bottom of a little valley. Comfortabl
and well thought-out interiors where each pen
sioner has a bedroom, a sitting room and a sma
kitchen of his own. Calm and restful surroun
dings, a miniature cloister which has becom
lay: one of the most lovable buildings in Londor
[Blackheath].

**Baroque churches.** In 1711, the new Tory government passed a law for the building of fifty churches in the expanding suburbs of London. Thus we see the three most important English Baroque architects, Hawksmoor, Archer and Gibbs, at work at the same period on the building of some of the twelve churches which were in fact actually completed. **Nicholas Hawksmoor** (1661-1736), after having been draughtsman to Wren for so many years, at the age of over fifty, finally had his chance. In little more than ten years he designed five churches: he builds, gouges, one might say, the façades and the towers of his churches with passionate conviction, and a vigour which reminds us of Michelangelo; his works are among the most original masterpieces of European Baroque. **Thomas Archer** (1668-1743) is the only English architect who, because he was almost certainly familiar at first hand with Italian architecture, could easily be placed in the Baroque tradition of Bernini and Borromini. Apart from Birmingham Cathedral, all his churches are in London. **James Gibbs** (1682-1754) is another architect in the Italian tradition; in fact he studied with Carlo Fontana in Rome from 1707 to 1709. It could be said that he had a double career, he began as a Baroque architect, only later to pass over to Palladianism, which had become fashionable in England, as these two churches of his, illustrated here, show.

**6**

**RANGERY, KENSINGTON PALACE, C. Wren ), 1704.** This Orangery in the gardens of Kensington Palace, where Wren designed part of the terior, with finely carved decorative details, is a tle jewel of brick architecture. The interior, with eat square windows looking S, consists of a ng gallery ending in two circular rooms. It is at-buted to Wren, but considering its Baroque eling it could have been designed by either anbrugh or Hawksmoor. [Kensington Gardens, yde Park].

Sir James Thornhill, Ceiling of the Painted Hall, Royal Hospital, Greenwich, 1707-1717.

a

c

## 37

**ST. GEORGE-IN-THE-EAST, N. Hawksmoo**
**1715-23.** Severely damaged during the last wa
only the tower and exterior have survived. The V
front rises to become a square tower on whos
flat surface the windows appear set into deep re
cesses. This angular tower is then crowned by
lantern almost Gothic in taste. This originality of
design verges on eccentricity, but it produce
unforgettable forms. [Cannon Street Road, Ste|
ney].

a  b

## 58

**ST. ANNE LIMEHOUSE, N. Hawksmoor, 1712-20.** Another extraordinary front with tower of a very complex design where each element, marked by buttresses in the form of square pilasters, fits into the next by means of large arches. The **portal**, inserted between two giant diagonal buttresses, like open arms, is formed by an apsidal semicircular projection with semidome. Solemn interior of austere simplicity. [Commercial Road, Stepney].

c

**39**
**ST. MARY WOOLNOTH, N. Hawksmoor, 1716-1727.** Façade decorated simply by banded rustication in which is set the great niche of the door. The tower, with a rectangular plan, presents a sort of loggia of three bays against a flat wall, the top is subdivided into two little square turrets. The sculptural quality of Hawksmoor's architecture appears clearly in the **side windows** (above) which repeat the motif of the rusticated niche. Very original and monumental interior, it is a square inside a square, the inner square top lit with great lunettes. [Bank, City].

**40**
**CHRIST CHURCH, SPITALFIELDS, N. Hawksmoor, 1723-9.** A very original portico formed by four Tuscan columns carrying a semicircular arch, behind it rises the wide, flat tower with concave sides, similar to gigantic niches where the windows are set in. This tower «has, as it were, wings, which gives it immense breath at the base, and it soars up to an almost Gothic spire» (Summerson). The interior repeats the St. James's scheme (29), but is vaster and more monumental. [Spitalfields, Stepney].

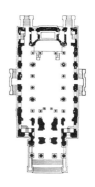

**1**

**T. JOHN SMITH SQUARE, T. Archer, 1713-28.**
 sincerely Baroque piece of architecture, the
 ore so because it is completely isolated in the
entre of a public square. Greek cross plan. The
vo side entrances have giant Tuscan columns
n antis», above there is a pediment open at the
p with a central aedicule. W front and apse
onsist of a vast Venetian window with attic, vo-
tes and pediment. Splendid circular turrets
rown the church at the four corners. Restored
fter serious war damage. [Smith Square, West-
inster].

**42**

**ST. PAUL DEPTFORD, T. Archer, 1712-30.** This
church presents a completely new solution to the
problem of incorporating portico and tower: the
semicircular portico carries a round tower, so
that the two elements are perfectly coherent with
each other. The curve of the portico, on the other
hand, recalls that of the apse. Magnificent staircases (badly in need of repair) surround the
church. The interior has an almost square plan
which appears oval because of the wide curve of
the apse. «One of the most moving XVIII c.
churches of London: large, sombre and virile»
(Pevsner). [High Street, Deptford].

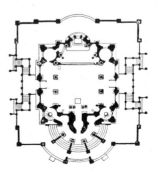

a

## 43

**ST. MARY-LE-STRAND, J. Gibbs, 1714-17.** This small church is a jewel of English Baroque architecture, «admirably placed on an island site in the Strand, and visible from all sides, as if it were a casket one can handle with one's hand» (Pevsner). W front with semicircular entrance porch; then, above the central window flanked by twin columns, rises the steeple which, with three stages of superimposed columns and pilasters, continues the vertical thrust of the entrance portico. Simple interior with coffered ceiling in the Italian style. [Strand].

d

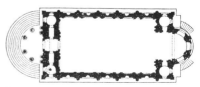

c

**44**

**T. MARTIN-IN-THE-FIELDS, J. Gibbs, 1722-26.**
ne of the most influential buildings in England,
church prototype imitated countless times in
e Anglo-Saxon world. It also marks the begin-
ng of the neo-Palladian or neo-classical, and
erefore anti-Baroque, period. St. Martin's is
een as a Greek temple on the roof of which, in a
ther uncomfortable manner, is planted the tow-
. The interior, which again follows the pattern of
t. James's (29), is splendidly decorated by
lasterwork, the masterpiece of two Italian
raftsmen, Giuseppe Artari and Pietro Bagutti.
he pulpit is exquisitely carved. The apse, with
oxes at the sides, has the sinuous elegance of a
ococo theatre. [Trafalgar Square].

**45**

**GROSVENOR CHAPEL, c. 1730.** This country-
like little church in the heart of London recalls the
rural origins of XVIII c. Mayfair, as does
Shepherd's Market nearby. It was built when
London started to develop N of Westminster with
the plans for Grosvenor Square (of which this
chapel is part), Berkeley Square, Hanover
Square, etc. This pretty building, with its small
porch and little tower with octagonal spire, can
be considered a typical example of colonial
style, very popular in North America (New England) during the XVIII c. [South Audley Street,
Mayfair].

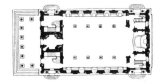

## GEORGIAN LONDON: PALLADIANISM AND NEO-CLASSICISM

The eighteenth century was one of aristocratic supremacy, with power concentrated in the hands of a few influential families. With the introduction of Cabinet Government the English monarchy saw its power definitively reduced. It is also the century of economic liberalism and colonial expansion. It was a golden century for the English aristocracy, which came unscathed through even the great fear of the French Revolution. Its only setback was the loss of the North American colonies in 1776.

**The Palladians.** The beginning of the eighteenth century was dominated by the Whig party, avowedly opposed to the preceding Stuart dynasty, with its authoritarian tradition, and therefore opposed too to what it had produced architecturally, i.e. Wren and the Baroque style. The anti-Baroque reaction found its ideals in Jones's Classical Palladian purism, sponsored with great success by **Lord Burlington** (1694-1753). Amongst the architects of his group **William Kent** (1685-1748) stands out, an architect who, however, continued to show clear Baroque leanings. He was, amongst other things, the inventor, it might be said, of the English style landscaped garden.

a

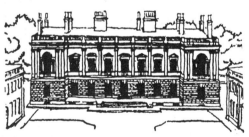

Burlington House, the façade in the original state, C. Campbell 1715-16.

## 46

**CHISWICK HOUSE, Lord Burlington, 1725-3(**
Lord Burlington designed Chiswick House soo
after returning from his second Italian tour,
homage to Palladio and a landmark in the histor
of English architecture. It is directly inspired b
Palladio's country houses (especially the Vill
Rotonda) and in part by Scamozzi (Villa Pisana
It was not the first neo-Palladian country hous
built in England (Mereworth by Campbell date
from 1723), but it was certainly the most influen
tial. The portico on the **main front** (c) and th
dome are clearly Palladian, though the doubl

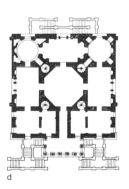

d

e

taircase leading to the portico shows a marked Baroque taste in its complexity. The interior, with s octagonal domed hall, appears rather fractioned and confused if we exclude the magnificent **gallery** (d) where the succession of the hree rooms is very well solved, considering the imited space available, especially attractive being the central room with apsed ends. The Baroque ornaments of the interiors, decorated by a series of paintings by Sebastiano Ricci, are designed by William Kent. No less important than he house in the history of taste is the **garden** (b)

laid out by Kent: it is the first important example of landscape gardening in the new picturesque style, a reaction to the exact geometry of the French Baroque gardens. This type of garden, inspired by the paintings of Claude Lorrain, tends to recreate a natural setting against which to place the classical architecture of the country house. Kent also designed the canal which, with its sinuous banks, runs through the garden from one end to the other, of the same period are also the little Ionic temple and the circular **pond** (a) with obelisk.

## 47

**MANSION HOUSE, G. Dance the Elder, 1739-53.**
The official residence of the Lord Mayor, this
building, with its classical portico, is a characteristic product of the neo-Palladian movement,
that is to say, an adaptation of the Venetian villa
to an English town palace; it is however, neither a
villa nor a palace, but homage to the fashion of
the period which is already academic in taste.
The interiors are remarkable, particularly the
spectacular Egyptian Room designed according
to the principles illustrated by Vitruvius. [Bank].

## 48

**HOUSE, No. 44 Berkeley Square, W. Kent, 174:
4.** The façade has simple and correct classica
proportions; the interior, on the other hand, dis
plays one of the most splendid inventions in En
glish architecture, the great staircase. «There i
no other XVIII c. staircase in England which ca
so convincingly be compared with those of th
great German and Austrian Baroque architects
(Pevsner). It occupies the whole height of th
building and, though contained in a rather limite
space, appears to be of majestic proportions
Between the first and the second floor it climb
behind a screen of Ionic columns ending on
curved bridge-like landing.

**9**

**HORSE GUARDS, W. Kent, 1745-60.** In this building Kent shows a clear Baroque inclination and he seems to have Vanbrugh as a model rather than Jones. The plan is extremely complex and the whole design is formed by an ingenious collection of cubes; both sides of the main block, the **W front**, towards Horse Guards Parade, and the front facing Whitehall (executed after Kent's death by John Vardy, who probably changed the original design), present projecting centre bays and are flanked by square turrets with pyramid roofs. The clock tower, crowned by an open lantern, is also very Baroque in feeling. [Whitehall].

**Neo-Classicism.** The Neo-Classical movement represents a new attitude to the past in general and to the art of classical antiquity in particular, which for the first time was studied at first hand, thanks to new archeological research. It was idealised as the perfect architectural expression, more simple, linear and rational in comparison with the excesses of the Baroque and Rococo tradition. In England the path had been smoothed by the Palladians; in fact **William Chambers** (1723-1796) is the heir to pure Palladianism and sometimes he lapses into mere academicism. **Robert Adam** (1728-92) is certainly a more original figure; taking his inspiration direct from Greek and Roman antiquities, he created a kind of marriage between Neo-Classicism and Rococo. Adam is above all a designer of interiors, and his work is of an extreme, almost effeminate, elegance. At the same time he is a real architect; in the succession of rooms typical of his style, he reveals himself to be a master of complex spatial effects. Of the architects following Adam, at last two must be mentioned, **Henry Holland** (1745-1806) and **George Dance the Younger** (1741-1825) who, as a reaction to some of Adam's excesses of decoration, further simplified the architecture of the period: a golden age which was to last until the first decades of the nineteenth century, when «never had standards of tastes and execution stood higher». (Summerson).

## 50

**MANRESA HOUSE, W. Chambers, c. 1760.** country house which witnesses the continuity o the Palladian style in the second half of the cen tury: Ionic portico with curved staircase and rus ticated basement, a very competent building an rather academic, in this sense more correctl Palladian than Chiswick House. Its particula charm is due to the magnificent position ove looking the open expanses of Richmond Park; thus becomes a prototype of the English XVIII c country house. At its back are visible the grea towers of the Alton West and Alton East estate (95). [Roehampton].

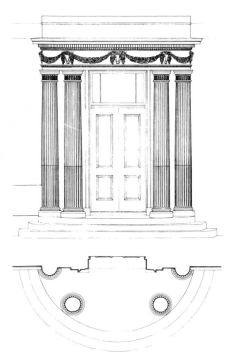

**A Neo-Classical Porch.** The Coade stone porch of Brunswick House, Albert Embankment, London SE1, dating from the 1780s in the style of Robert Adam. Drawing by Peter Wyld from «London: The Art of Georgian Building».

**1**

**SOMERSET HOUSE, W. Chambers, 1776-86.**
The basic idea of his huge palace, the most important of Chambers' works, is very similar to the Adelphi (57), designed eight years earlier by the Adam brothers. It is the largest classical public building in England after Greenwich; it was erected to house a number of government offices and learned societies. Behind the classical Palladian façade towards the Strand there is a vast quadrangle surrounded by ranges of buildings of a similar design. The **S front**, overlooking the Thames, is the most monumental and spectacular part of the scheme, in front of it runs a long terrace (800 ft) which rests on a series of rusticated arches. The composition of the façade proper is subdivided by three open colonnades, the side ones being supported by giant arches, a motif inspired by Piranesi. To E and W there are the XIX century extensions by Robert Smirke (1821-1835), the King's College, and by James Pennethorne (1859). [Strand].

Somerset House, N front towards the Strand.

a

b

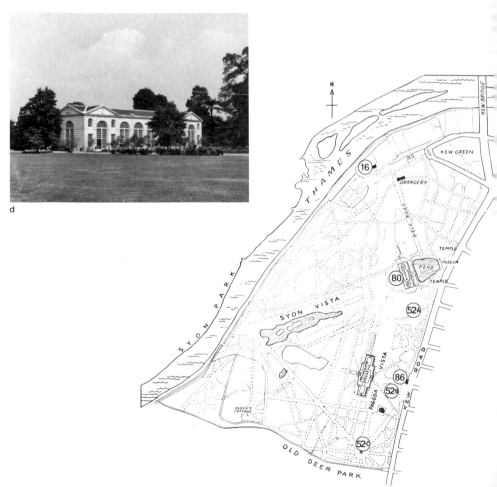

d

## 52

**EW GARDENS, ORNAMENTAL BUILDINGS, W. hambers, 1760-63.** The most beautiful and largest (300 acres in size) botanic garden in the world, an extraordinary place not only for its scientific interest and the beauty of the varied landscape, but also for the quality of the buildings which include the Kew Palace (18), Chambers' ornamental works, the Palm House (80) and Nesfield's Lodge (86). The present garden dates from different periods; it was designed by Chambers, first of all, and Capability Brown (the Rhododendron Dell, 1773), then, towards the middle of the XIX c. the picturesque lake and the pond were excavated. Kew Gardens can be said to form a compendium of the English art of landscape gardening. Of the Chambers buildings still standing are three little temples, those of **Bellona** (a), Aeolus and Arethusa, the **Ruined Arch** (b) and the **Pagoda** (c). They are a fascinating collection, illustrating the taste of the period, neoclassic, but already eclectic, in the lighthearted spirit of the Rococo. Even Chambers' Palladian armour was not so thick after all.

## 53

**STRAWBERRY HILL, produced by H. Walpole, 1750-72.** The classical-oriental mid-XVIII c. anthology by Chambers at Kew is here completed with the gothic component. This celebrated residence of Horace Walpole, built by different architects under the supervision of the writer, is one of the earliest and most influential neo-gothic buildings in the history of European architecture: the Middle Ages rebuilt in a spirit which is romantic and Rococo at the same time. The house, completely asymmetrical, preserves in its exterior too that toy-like aspect, as if it were a three dimensional stage design, which fascinated its owner much. The most charming room inside is certainly the staircase «so pretty and so small – wrote Walpole to a friend – that I am inclined to wrap it up and send it you in my letter». [Waldegrave Road, Twickenham].

## 54

**HOME HOUSE, R. Adam, 1774-6.** One of the most beautiful houses in London, now the Courtauld Institute of Art (University of London). The façade presents only a few restrained ornaments (garlands), while the interior displays a beautiful series of rooms finely decorated with stucco and paintings by Antonio Zucchi and Angelica Krauffmann. The magnificent **staircase**, which occupies the whole height of the building and is lit by a circular skylight, can only be compared to that by Kent in Berkeley Square (48). [Portman Square].

## 55

**SYON HOUSE, R. Adam, 1761.** Another Tud● building altered by Adam in the years he w● working at Osterley Park. We have here a spect● cular sequence of five rooms which begins wi● the imposing Entrance Hall, an apsed «doub● cube» containing copies of ancient statues; th● is followed by the sumptuous **Ante Room**, dec● rated by twelve «verde antico» columns place● against pale green walls; then the Dining Roo● with screened-off apses, white and gold; aft● this the red Drawing Room; finally the Great G● lery, 136 ft long, decorated by different classic● motifs, in a mauve and pale green colo● scheme. For the variety of spatial effects and t● splendour of its ornaments this is probab● Adam's masterpiece, where «the hall, the stai● case, each room, each closet, fits into a counte● point of living-space; every wall of every roo● has been caressed in the architect's mind ar● persuaded into a delicate discipline mutually e● hancing that of the rooms before and beyond i● (Summerson).

## 6

**OSTERLEY PARK, R. Adam, 1761-72.** A country house of Tudor origin remodelled by Adam from 1761 onwards, that is to say at the same time as Syon House. He redesigned almost all interiors and part of the exterior, adding the classical portico which links the inner courtyard with the gardens: «the effect with the slim unfluted Ionic columns is as delicate and celestial and as chastely theatrical as any opera Gluck might have composed in these very same years». (Pevsner).

The entrance hall.

## 57

**ROYAL SOCIETY OF ARTS, R. Adam, 1772-4.** It was part of the Adelphi, the most important classical complex ever built in central London (demolished between 1872 and 1936) and which inspired Chambers' Somerset House (50). This beautiful façade, with four Ionic columns and pediment, has, at the centre, a Venetian window crowned by a typical Adam fan. [John Adam Street, Strand].

View of the Adelphi in an 18th century print, S front towards the Thames.

## 58

**KEN WOOD HOUSE, R. Adam, 1766.** Hampstea and Highgate, with their narrow, winding street climbing steeply through gardens and ope spaces, still today give an impression of moun tain villages; in the XVIII c they were in fact sun mer resorts for Londoners. Between these tw centres, facing Hampstead Heath, is Ken Woo an early XVIII c. country house remodelled b Adam in 1766. It is certainly the most importan building in this part of London, also because its exceptional collection of paintings (Ren brandt, Vermeer, Guardi, Boucher, Gainsbc rough, Turner, etc.). Adam added the entranc portico and the orangery on the W side and red signed part of the interior. His masterpiece is th beautiful **Library** which has screened-off apse at both ends, tunnel vault and walls covered wi stucco ornaments and paintings by Zucch [Hampstead Lane].

**9**

**LL HALLOWS, LONDON WALL, G. Dance the ounger, 1765-7.** Built by Dance when he was nly twenty-four, just returned from his travels in aly and France. Nave without aisles and cof- ered apse, the tunnel vault is supported by Ionic olumns placed against the outer walls, there is o entablature, a frieze marks the upper limits of ne walls; high semicircular windows, set in the enetrations of the vault, are the only openings. his purification of structural elements and de- orative details was to influence John Soane reatly, who was to become the revolutionary naster of neoclassicism in the early XIX c. [Lon- on Wall].

**60**

**CHAPEL, GREENWICH HOSPITAL, J. Stuart, 1779.** Masterpiece of the neo-Grecian style, whose most influential representative was in fact James Stuart, called the Athenian. He was also the author of the first book on Greek architecture (Antiquities of Athens, 1762). Segmental vault and sumptuous church, and, at the same time, ri- gidly disciplined. Altar painting by Benjamin West. Splendid circular pulpit.

a

b

## 61

**DOVER HOUSE, H. Holland, 1787.** The exquisit
and minute proportions of the Ionic portic
placed against the plain wall, and in perfect rela
tion to the dome above the vestibule, make th
architecture as precious as a Wedgwood vase
The **vestibule** (b), lit from the glazed dome, is als
of a remarkable elegance with its circle of Tus
can columns in pink marble, and the semicircu
lar steps. A voluminous plinth with a military f
gure on top, placed in the middle of the road, ur
fortunately spoils the best view of this civilise
building from the opposite pavement of White
hall. A monumental reminder, perhaps, of wha
Pietro Aretino said: «The soldier is like the whore
Both are paid to do evil». [Whitehall].

**2**

**ICHMOND BRIDGE, J. Paine & K. Couse, 1774-**
. The only XVIII c. Thames bridge left in the Lon-
on region. Elegant and majestic in the simple
eometry of its five graduated arches and semi-
irculat buttresses, this bridge fits perfectly in the
reen river landscape of Richmond and suits the
ace admirably. Richmond is a village which
reserves intact numerous XVIII c. features, such
s the Green, Richmond Hill towards Petersham,
ichmond Park, etc., which seem to have
hanged little in the last couple of centuries.

**63**

**HOUSE IN CLOTH FAIR, late XVII c.** A rare and
picturesque example of a late XVII c. house. With
its large, square wooden bay-windows and
steep pitched roof with dormers, it is a type of
building which represents a moment of transition
between Tudor domestic architecture and the
extremely restrained one of the XVIII c. [West
Smithfield].

## 64

**HOUSES IN QUEEN ANNE'S GATE, c. 1704.**
From the beginning of the XVIII c. the London
house is almost a standardised product, plain
brick front with no pediment, square sash windows; only the doors sometimes have elaborate
ornaments, such as the wooden canopies in the
Baroque taste of the examples here illustrated.
[Westminster].

## 65

**HOUSES IN LOWER MALL, Hammersmith, la**
**XVIII c.** «Mall», according to the Oxford Diction
ary, is a «sheltered walk as promenade»; a pe
fectly suitable description of this riverside, one
the most charming along the Thames, which
here almost a country stream. A number of thes
late XVIII c. houses have the pretty iron veranda
which became fashionable at that time.

**THE PARAGON, c. 1790.** A very civilised and original example of refined late XVIII c. domestic architecture. Seven perfectly identical four-storey units, linked by a curved colonnade, form a crescent overlooking Blackheath. At the **back** (b) each unit has two semicircular projections. This cubic and cylindric geometry gives an almost XX flavour to the building and shows how its designer was up to date with the purist taste of the period. [Blackheath].

b

# THE TWO FACES OF THE NINETEENTH CENTURY

The XIX century is the period of England's greatest colonial and industrial expansion. It is also a century of striking political and social contradictions. Contradictory too is the architecture of the period, and not only in England, of course; but England, and perhaps London more than any other city in Europe, preserves some of the most significant examples of this century.

The architecture of the early XIX century achieves a functionalism and a purity of form admirably suited to the first great industrial structures and to the use of the new building materials, iron and glass. Then comes the «fancy-dress ball of architecture» typical of the Victorian age. In the second half of the century some English artists succeed in finding a new and original style free of imitations which was to place them in the forefront of the pioneers of modern architecture and design.

**Regency.** The Regency style belongs to those early decades of the century when architecture seems to sum up what was best in the XVIII century tradition. The two key figures are John Nash, who brought the Picturesque movement to its most advanced solutions still considered valid for the planners of today, and John Soane, who even further purified Neo-Classical geometry evolving an almost XX century style. But the architecture of the period does not end with these two exceptional figures, as will be seen, and many other builders, sometimes anonymous, co tribute to the characteristic face of Regency Lo don.

**Sir John Soane** (1753-1837). The most origir English architect after Hawksmoor, with whc he seems to have a certain affinity, and one of t most significant representatives in Europe functional, or rationalist classicism, following t trend pioneered by Ledoux and other French a chitects of the Age of Reason. He thus belongs that group of architects who, at the turn of t century, can already be considered the for runners of modern functionalism, that sty which Le Corbusier made the most characteri ic of our times. But like Le Corbusier, Soar knew how to break out of strictly defined theori in order to create a new and personal style. Pe sonal to the point of perversity, his style has fact been called; it is made up of curiously d tached elements though always related to t elementary geometrical unit on which his bu dings are always based. He was a pupil of Dan and Holland, who gave him a first-class profe sional training, and when thirty years old he d signed his masterpiece, the **Bank of Englar** (see print reproduced on page 81), demolishe 1921-37. In later years he developed even mo freely, producing two of the most outstanding original buildings in Europe, the Dulwich Art Ga lery and his own house in London.

Sir John Soane, Mausoleum to Mrs Soane, St. Pancras, Old Parish Church, 1815.

## 67

**STABLES, CHELSEA HOSPITAL, J. Soane, 1814-1817.** A plain, utilitarian brick building; the geometrical precision of the arches gives it an extraordinary energy. «It is far more comprehensible to the abstract tastes of the twentieth century than in accordance with the ideals most widely accepted in the England of Soane's own day» (H.R. Hitchcock). See also no. 31.

(a) Detail of the façade

## 68
**DULWICH ART GALLERY, J. Soane, 1811-14.**
This consists of the long, low building of the gallery proper, with the small **Mausoleum**, or funerary chapel, for the donors of the collection in the middle. A building studied and executed with utmost, almost fanatical care in its subtlest details. «Observe how carefully each element is given quasi-independence of its neighbour, chiefly by the device of making slight recessions in the plan where small entrance lobbies are introduced. This produces a curious tension throughout the design, each part bearing a distinct and intense relationship to the whole ... the building as a whole reaches a level of emotional eloquence and technical performance rare in English, or indeed in European architecture». (Summerson).

## 69
**SIR JOHN SOANE'S MUSEUM, J. Soane, 181 14.** This is the house that Soane built for himse it preserves his private collection of painting drawings and sculpture. This building preser practically no traditional classical motifs and appears to be almost a product of the Vienne Secession. The interiors are subdivided with continuous search for spatial effects obtained the most unconventional manner, by means domes, hanging arches and mirrors, as in tl **Breakfast Room** (c), and exploiting the differe levels of the floors. [Lincoln's Inn Fields].

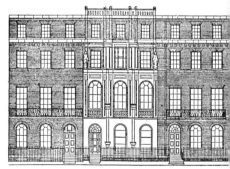

(b) Front towards Lincoln's Inn Fields

The Breakfast Room

) An interior of the Bank of England (altered 1925) by Sir John
Soane, 1818

## 70

**ST. JOHN BETHNAL GREEN, J. Soane, 1825-8.**
The most successful of Soane's church designs,
it presents one of the best solutions of the eternal
problem of combining W façade and tower. The
front is divided into three squares by two deep
fissures where the side doors are set. The tower,
another symmetrical cube, acquires its independence by having detached pillars at the angles.
Interiors completely rebuilt. [Cambridge Heath
Road].

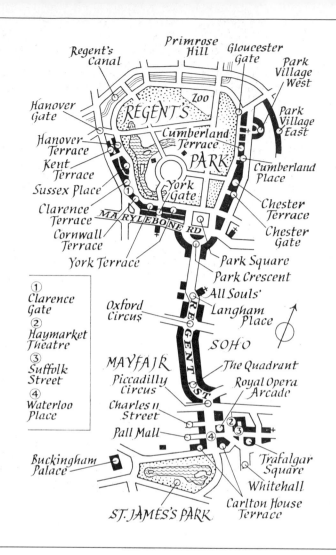

By courtesy London Transport

**John Nash** (1752-1835). The most successfu architect of early XIX century. He began his car rer in London under Robert Taylor and was late a partner of Humphry Repton, the landscap gardener. In association with Repton he built nu merous country houses in a variety of styles bringing the Picturesque movement to its mos fanciful and attractive expressions. A prolific an original builder (he was among the first archi tects to design houses with an asymmetrica plan), he is remembered above all as the grea planner of London and can be considered th initiator of the idea of the garden-city.

Park Village West

# 1

**HE REGENT'S PARK-REGENT STREET PLAN,
Nash, 1811-26.** John Nash was already sixty
hen he was commissioned to design the most
portant planning project ever conceived for
ondon: the development of Marylebone Park,
ter Regent's Park, and St. James's Park, and
e layout of a new street, Regent Street, which
as to link the two parks crossing through the
entre of the capital. In this enormous scheme,
ompleted in a little over fifteen years, Nash
ows an inexhaustible invention both from an
rchitectural and a town-planning point of view.
ometimes his buildings seem to be little more
an stage scenery, and just about as substan-
al, but they are always designed with a precise
ense of mass and space to achieve the most
easant and unexpected result in terms of
wnscape. He in fact made «the most ingenious
se of that principle of picturesque planning:
urprise» (Pevsner). The Regent's Park plan, be-
des the terraces to be built around the area,
cluded a garden-city in the middle of the park,
omposed of twenty-six villas, a pleasure pavi-
on for the Regent and church; on the E side two
nall residential centres with shops and markets
t the back. In the end only eight villas were built
side the park, but in **Park Village West** (a/b)
ash designed one of the first garden-cities,
ough in miniature, or rather the earliest
xample of a garden suburb: houses of various
tyles line a winding street with plenty of green-
ry; less well preserved is Park Village East. The
egent's Canal, N of the park, is crossed by the
**acclesfield Bridge** (c) built by a Nash assistant,
ames Morgan: three brick arches resting on
ast-iron Doric columns; a tough, functional
tructure interpreted with classical motifs which
ecalls a design made by Ledoux for his Maison
u Plaisir. The white stuccoed terraces along the

(b) Park Village West

(c) Macclesfield Bridge

(d) Chester Terrace

(e) Chester Terrace

(f) All Souls Church

perimeter remain practically intact, externally  least: ten huge buildings of different lengths an complexity, all in the Neo-Classical style, vague ly Palladian, decorated by porticoes, arches, pe diments and statues. Those on the E side ar particularly imposing such as **Chester Terrac** (d/e) and, above all, **Cumberland Terrace** (g «easily the most breath-taking architectural pa norama in London» (Summerson). To the S th park is connected with Portland Place (built b Adam in 1774) through Park Square and **Par Crescent** (h). At the end of Portland Place, t mark the change of direction, Nash erected th circular colonnade of the church of **All Souls** ( From here Regent Street proper continue straight down to the wide sweep of the Quadra before reaching Piccadilly Circus. Then, anothe straight run led to St. James's Park. Today almo nothing remains of Nash's Regent Street, whic was completely rebuilt in 1905-25. After Rege Street and the imposing façade of **Carlton Hous Terrace** (m), Nash redesigned **St. James's Par** (l) according to the picturesque principles o landscape gardening. But this was not all: Nash work extended to the side streets of Rege Street, Haymarket, where he built the theatr **Suffolk Street** (n) and Pall Mall East with th Royal Opera Arcade. He also planned Trafalga Square, as we know it today, including the begin ning of the **Strand** (i) with the circular turre which still stand at the corner of Adelaide Stree

Cumberland Terrace

Park Crescent

(i) Corner of Adelaide Street and the Strand

(l) St. James's Park

(m) Carlton House Terrace, St. James's Park

(n) Suffolk Street

**2**

**LOYD SQUARE, 1819.** The other face of Reg-
ncy London. Just as Belgrave Square, with its
rand design, is obviously aristocratic in charac-
r, Lloyd Square is utilitarian, intimate, middle
ass. It is composed of terraces of small semi-
etached houses; their simple, cubic brick
.ructure, lined by white bands, almost recall the
orutalistic» style of today, though they preserve
typically classical sense of proportion. [Fins-
ury].

**73**

**BELGRAVIA, T. Cubitt, c. 1825.** Among the great
development schemes of the early XIX c.
(Bloomsbury, also by Thomas Cubitt, Paddington, Islington, etc.) Belgravia is certainly the most
spectacular, besides being the one best preserved. It is a typical expression of the Regency
period under the direct influence of Nash. The
plan includes three squares: Belgrave Square,
Eaton Square and Chester Square, all with central gardens and connected by wide streets. Architecturally they follow the models of Regent's
Park, each side of the square being a uniform
range of Classical stuccoed houses decorated
by porticoes, columns, pilasters and pediments.
**Belgrave Square** is the most attractive and one of
the most typical of all London squares.

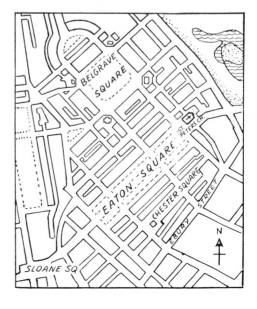

## 74

**KEATS HOUSE, c. 1815.** A characteristic Regency house where the poet John Keats lived between 1818 and 1820. A very pure design: white stuccoed façade; the windows of the ground floor are enclosed within an arch, on the upper floor they almost touch the roof line; projecting eaves on thin iron brackets; the chimney stack is built as a flat, square shape as high as the house itself. Voysey's architecture almost seems to have originated here. The left wing was added in 1838. Various houses of the same period are to be found in Keats' Grove and the nearby Downshire Hill; one the most charming parts of London, gathered around the small, delightful Neo-Classical chapel of St. John. [Hampstead].

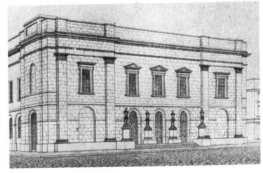

## 75

**VOBURN WALK, T. Cubitt, c. 1822.** Shopfronts esigned as part of the façade of the building of which they formed the base were first built during he Regency. One of the best surviving examples f a designed shopping street is Woburn Walk by homas Cubitt, the developer of Bloomsbury and elgravia. Each unit is marked by a slight reces- ion of the wall and each shop-window is flanked y two doors, one giving access to the shop, the ther to the house above. [Bloomsbury].

## 76

**DRURY LANE THEATRE, B. Wyatt, 1810-12.** The best example in London of a Theatre of the Clas- sical period. Wyatt's building has been pre- served intact, both interior and exterior, except for the addition of the portico and the Ionic colon- nade at the side which were added in 1820 and 1831 respectively. Beautiful interior, particularly the first floor **foyer** with circular balcony under the dome.

**Iron, glass and functional architecture.** The Industrial Revolution, which in England began at the end of the XVIII century, created the need for new types of strictly functional buildings, such as factories, bridges, warehouses, markets, railway stations, etc. At the same time, iron, which for the first time was produced on a large scale, offered builders entirely new possibilities. Early industrial buildings were often designed by engineers and not by architects, though they found in functional classicism of the period forms which were perfectly suitable to their needs. The fact that these buildings, even when they have no aesthetic ambitions, «are in fact pleasing to our eyes is due to the many good qualities they share with other buildings in the functional tradition of whatever period. They have a clarity of form and a subtle modelling of solid and voids that many works of architecture of a more sophisticated origin might envy... Then there is their expressive use of materials and their trimness of detail. In fact they display, unobscured by the irrelevances of ornament, the essential attributes of architecture» (J.M. Richards). Some of the earliest and best iron and glass structures are still in existence in London, those by Fowler for instance, besides the extraordinary Palm House at Kew. Finally there are the railway sheds of Paddington and St. Pancras. But here we notice already the separation of tasks between the engineer, who is responsible for the iron structure, and the architect, who designs the station building according to the eclectic taste of the period.

J. Paxton, The Crystal Palace, 1851.

## 77

**ST. KATHARINE DOCKS, T. Telford, 1825-8.** The St. Katharine Docks, like the West India Docks, the London Docks and the Surrey Docks, were built at beginning of the XIX c. to meet the increasing trade of the port of London. They are purely functional structures, designed in fact by engineers such as John Rennie and Thomas Telford. Made of bricks with columns of iron or granite, the walls of these «great warehouses are lightened by arched recesses in which the windows are set, adding rhythm and grace to the strength and dignity common to all these early dock buildings» (J.M. Richards). Towards the basin the walls are built flush to the water's edge with regular recesses for the cranes. The N-E corner of St. Katharine Docks was destroyed during the war and the site is now occupied by a new and very good **office building** by Andrew Renton (1964).

## 78

**COVENT GARDEN MARKET, C. Fowler, 1828-31.** The earliest covered market of this type in London and still used. A building of remarkable elegance where the glass and iron structure of the roof is perfectly integrated with the neoclassical exterior with its side colonnade and corner lodges. Fowler «developed the vocabulary of iron-arched sheds, pillared concourses and subservient offices which in less than a decade was to personify the railway station» (Nicholas Taylor). The Floral Market, on the N-E corner of the square, is a more ornate building of iron and glass by E.M. Barry of 1859.

## 79

**GREENHOUSE, SYON HOUSE, C. Fowler, c. 1830.** Charles Fowler, the designer of Covent Garden Market, built this greenhouse, a Palladian capriccio in iron and glass, for the gardens of Syon House; it repeats in fact faithfully the pattern of the Venetian villa, with dome and curved wings. «The central rotunda is a vegetable dance, far removed from Paxton's seriousness. The huge iron columns seem to have been intended from the first to be covered with foliage, so this wonderful Schubertian frolic looks back to the eighteenth-century follies and forward to the Crystal Palace all at once. A golden moment, combining the taste of one century and the enterprise of the next» (Ian Nairn).

## 80

**PALM HOUSE, KEW GARDENS, R. Turner, 1844-8.** The Palm House is one of the earliest buildings in iron and glass and one of the most extraordinary in the history of European architecture, «much bolder and hence aesthetically much more satisfying than the Crystal Palace ever was» (Pevsner). It is 362 ft long, in the centre 62 ft and in the wings 33 ft high, it was designed by the Irish engineer Richard Turner as a greenhouse for tropical plants. This function has clearly determined its shape, since a greenhouse of this type needs a very hot and humid atmosphere: while the curved glass walls reduce the dispersion of heat, they allow a better exploitation of the sun's rays; moreover they let the condensed steam run down, eliminating any dripping. A pioneer building if ever there was one and the designer appears to have been in that state of grace that only one attempting something entirely new seems to possess. The Palm House erected, as we have seen, for purely functional reasons, has thus the purity of line of the best industrial designs, such as the aeroplane, where it is the function which dictates the shape; at the same time it has the essential quality and the coriaceous solidity of a creation of nature, such as the egg; seen against the light it acquires the springy elasticity of a vegetable membrane.

St. Pancras Station

(c) Paddington Station

St. Pancras Station

(d) Kings Cross Station

**RAILWAY STATIONS, Paddington Station,** (1850) is one of the earliest station sheds, it was designed by the great Victorian engineer Isambard K. Brunel; the ornamental parts are by the architect M.D. Wyatt. It is quite different from any other building of the same type, because of the complexity of spatial effects and the sense of lightness given to the structure by the meeting of the three sheds (the fourth, to the right, is a modern addition) and the «transept» at right angles halfway down the platforms. **St. Pancras Station** (1868-74), is a typical Victorian building in the mixture of functionalism (the shed) and extravagant Gothic ornaments (the station building and hotel). The shed, designed by W.H. Barlow and one of the largest ever built, has a span of 243 ft and a lenght of 690 ft. Sir George Gilbert

Scott's station and hotel is certainly the most Gothic among Victorian buildings, its skyline shows an unprecedented collection of gables, pinnacles and turrets. But Scott knew also how to design the eminently functional carriage ramp for the station entrance. Next to St. Pancras is the earlier **Kings Cross Station** (1851-2) by Lewis Cubitt, a completely different conception expressed in Neo-classical terms. «The great glory of the station is the front, with its two enormous stock-brick arches that close the ends of the sheds towards the Euston Road. The idea had been Duquesney's at the Gare de l'Est, but here there is no irrelevant Renaissance detail, only grand scale and clear expression of the arched spaces behind» (H.R. Hitchcock).

**Neo-Gothic.** The neo-Gothic tradition can be traced back to Wren and Hawksmoor, but it is difficult here to say whether these buildings are the earliest examples of Gothic Revival or the last expressions of Gothic Survival. Certainly various XVIII century buildings by William Kent and other architects, including that delightful folly which is Strawberry Hill, are Neo-Gothic, but these buildings are fundamentally exercises in ornamental architecture and stylistically not very correct. About 1840, through the efforts of such scholars and artists as Pugin and Ruskin, Gothic architecture was studied with scientific, archaeological thoroughness and extolled as the style best suited to the age for reasons that were, at the same time, historical, technical and religious. Neo-Gothic was without doubt the most popular style in Victorian England also because of its romantic and literary association. But soon other styles were enthusiastically adopted by different architects in quick succession, Renaissance, Baroque, Norman, and so on. This «fancy-dress ball» of all styles continued well into our own century.

**82**

**HOUSES OF PARLIAMENT, C. Barry and A. P**gin, 1835-60. The earliest and largest Neo-Goth ic building, and certainly the most famous. Th principal assistant to the architect Charles Bar was Auguste Pugin, artist, scholar and archite a fanatical supporter of the Gothic revival. If Bar produced the basic architectural conception the building, it was Pugin who designed wi inexhaustible invention all the innumerable d corative details of both the exterior and the int riors and most of the fitments. His princip source of inspiration was the Henry VII Chap (10). Seen from a distance the Houses of Parli ment have the fabulous appearance of a fair tale castle, a romantic Gothic fantasy.

The frontispiece of «Apology for the Revival of Christian Architecture in England» by A.W.N. Pugin, 1843.

**84**

**WER BRIDGE, 1886-94.** Another grand struc-
e which ought to have been strictly functional
effect, with its twin drawbridges, it is an enor-
us machine to cross the river) and which in-
ad has become, marked as it is as a medieval
stle, pure stage scenery. «But at night it is
gnificent. Intermittently lit, tremendously bul-
the pompous trimmings concealed and the
ge suspending cables emphasized: one of
se high points which lose nothing through be-
frankly melodramatic» (I. Nairn). The XIX cen-
y had certainly the genius for self-illusion.

**ALL SAINTS, MARGARET STREET, W. Butter-
field, 1849-59.** The small church of All Saints,
built between 1849-59 by William Butterfield in a
side street of Marylebone, is one of the most typical High Victorian churches. Its gothic style is very original, including German and – apparently –
Italian elements (in 1849, Ruskin had published
«The Seven Lamps of Architecture»). The building, comprising the church and rectory, is dominated by a very tall steeple, it is of dark red bricks
with stone enrichments. The lofty, short three
bays interior is decorated with a variety of ornamental elements, polychrome marble, coloured
tiles, gilding, stained glass, in the most heavily
Victorian fashion. Butterfield's style, «forceful
and powerful» (Pevsner), was to influence considerably the work of Philip Webb (no. 85) and the
Arts and Crafts Movement. [Margaret Street,
Marylebone].

**From Arts and Crafts to Art Nouveau.** William Morris (1834-96), reacting against heavy-handed Victorian standards of industrial production, created in 1861, with some Pre-Raphaelite friends, a workshop for the making of wall-papers, textiles, carpets, stained glass, etc., in highly stylised designs which contrasted strongly with the prevailing naturalist taste. Through his example and impassioned teaching he strongly influenced, particularly after the formation of the Arts and Crafts Exhibition Society, architects and designers not only in England but also abroad (such as the Belgian Van den Velde and the Deutscher Werkbund). At the same time the buildings by Philip Webb, which reflect Morris' teachings in architecture, helped to establish that new style that was later much more variedly expressed in the work of Norman Shaw and Voysey. The movement Morris founded, by refusing historical imitations, was to contribute considerably to the origins of Art Nouveau and modern architecture in Europe.

William Morris, The «Daisy» wallpaper, 1861.

(a) Red House, the courtyard

Edward Burne-Jones, Mosaic of the Annunciation in the Church of St. Paul by G.E. Street in Rome, 1881-98.

(c) Plan of the Red House

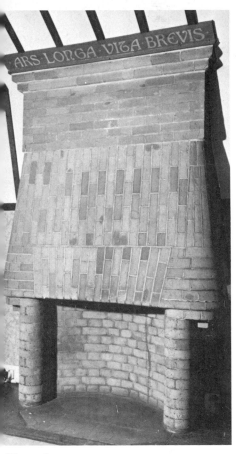

Chimney-piece

**ED HOUSE, P. Webb, 1859.** A famous and sig-ificant building, the house built by Philip Webb 1859 for William Morris. «It did in fact represent complete a revolution in English house design Inigo Jones' Queen's House at Greenwich of 518, though, of course, of a reserve order: in-ead of Anglicizing an alien mode it initiated a turn to the English rural tradition, and to craft-anship in native materials as a source of style stead of the Venetian Gothic or grandiose ench Renaissance then fashionable» (J.M. Ri-ards). The simplification in the architectural mposition is even clearer in certain interior de-ils, such as the **chimney-piece** (b) here illus-ated. [Red House Lane, Bexleyheath].

## 86

**LODGE, KEW GARDENS, E. Nesfield, 1866.** This charming brick lodge, with its steep pyramid roof and tall central chimney stack, goes back to the traditional late XVII c. architecture, which in turn was influenced by the Dutch Renaissance (27). It is one of the earliest and most original examples of that free traditionalism taught by Morris and Webb and it started the so-called Queen Anne fashion in domestic architecture which, taken up by Norman Shaw, a partner of Nesfield, lasted well into the XX century.

## 87

**SWAN HOUSE, N. Shaw, 1875.** Norman Shaw was the most prolific architect of the late XIX c. He began under the influence of Morris, Webb and Nesfield and in certain buildings which go back to traditional XVII c. architecture, such as Swan House and the adjacent Cheyne House (1876) in Chelsea, he shows remarkable discipline in the free treatment of picturesque motifs (63). He also designed, in 1875, the earliest Garden suburb in Bedford Park (88). In his later work he became heavier and heavier in style, ending up with the pompously Edwardian Piccadilly Hotel of 1905, which started the destruction of Nash's Regent Street. [Chelsea Embankment].

## 88

**HOUSE IN BEDFORD PARK, C.F. Voysey, 189** Bedford Park was laid out by Norman Shaw 1875. Voysey's house was built in 1891, it is th one of his earliest works, designed clearly contrast with Shaw's picturesque clichés. T slim, finely proportioned it is in the spirit of Nouveau; without superfluous decorative e ments and avoiding any reference to past styl it can be included among the very first truly m dern buildings (Charnley House in Chicago b by Wright when still working with Sullivan dat from the same year). [14 South Parade].

**9**

**'UDIO, C.F. Voysey, 1891.** Though nearer to ditional sources, in this Studio, which was ilt in the same year as the Bedford Park house, ysey again shows remarkable independence style. Typical of Voysey are the flat buttresses, e massive chimney stack, the projecting roof pported, as in Bedford Park, by thin iron bra- ets and, particularly, the refined iron railing ich recalls the work of Mackintosh of a few ars later. [St. Dunstan's Road, Hammersmith].

**90**

**WHITECHAPEL ART GALLERY, C.H. Townsend, 1895-9.** Townsend is certainly, together with Mackintosh, the main representative of Art Nou- veau in Britain, they in fact worked at practically the same period producing some of the most original buildings of that period in Europe. The Whitechapel Gallery was certainly influenced by Voysey, and the asymmetrical arched doorway by H.H. Richardson, the great American pioneer of modern architecture who was in London in 1885 (and built Lululand House in Bushey, Hert- fordshire). The Gallery was renovated in 1985 and a major extension added at the rear by ar- chitects Colquhoun and Miller. This work was accomplished with great skill.

## 91

**HORNIMAN MUSEUM, C.H. Townsend, 1900-1902.** An even bolder building than the previous one, particularly the massive tower with its rounded corners and round pinnacles: it seems to foreshadow an expressionist type of architecture. [London Road, Forest Hill].

## TWENTIETH CENTURY ARCHITECTURE: A SERVICE TO SOCIETY

The most promising architects of the late ) century ended their career rather sadly: Voys practically stopped work at the beginning of t century, and Norman Shaw became pompou Edwardian in his later buildings. Also the peri between the two wars was not very creative Britain, in spite of the fact that a number of fi class architects, such as Walter Gropius, fo while, Maxwell Fry, Berthold Lubetkin, Char Holden, etc., worked there during that peri( The true renaissance of modern architecture Britain is a post-war phenomenon. In 1945 t Labour Government severely limited building a tivity giving priority to housing and schools. At t same time the London County Council put tog ther a team of architects who produced, duri those years, «some of the finest housing a some of the finest schools in Europe» (G.E. K der Smith). Standardisation and prefabricati have been adopted on a much larger scale th in other countries. But British contemporary a chitecture is not only technically up to date, i often conceived with great imagination, partic larly where planning is concerned. The buildi of the new towns, eight as satellites of London another outstanding example of the great vital of British architecture today, which is seen not a luxury for a few but as a service to society as whole.
After the Brutalistic period, represented by Der Lasdun and the group of architects working the LCC, when Le Corbusier's influence was f more strongly, the architecture of London h reflected most of the new fashions which ha become popular recently in Europe, from t High Tech architecture of Richard Roge (Lloyd's Building) and Norman Foster (Fred ( sen Line Terminal), to the so called Post Mode nism of Venturi-Rauch-Scott Brown at the Sain bury Wing of the National Gallery. But perha the most original buildings of the Eighties are Sir Hugh Casson and James Stirling (see nos. and 99). They are rather small in size, but, aft all, the scale of architecture in London is mu smaller, more intimate, than that of other great ( ties, Rome or Paris, for instance. London is ce tainly not a city of palaces, of monumental bu dings; up to the beginning of the last century was not a city at all, but, as it has been said, a cc lection of villages, and this is still today one of th most fascinating aspects of its urban enviro ment.

## 2

**IGHPOINT FLATS, B. Lubetkin, 1933-38.** These
vo tower blocks, Highpoint One and Highpoint
vo, built between 1935 and 1938, by the Tecton
roup under the direction of Berthold Lubetkin,
e among the finest buildings of this type in Eu-
pe in the inter-war period. Le Corbusier des-
ibed them as a «vertical garden city». They
ake the most of their panoramic position in one
highest parts of Highgate. Built of reinforced
oncrete on «pilotis», Number One is seven sto-
ys high, each storey contains eight flats; they
e very well preserved today. Other works in
ngland of this Russian architect include several
avilions of the Zoo in Regent's Park (the pen-
iin pool with its reinforced concrete ramps is
articularly remarkable) built in the period 1934-
8 when Julian Huxley was the Zoo's director.
North Hill, Highgate].

## 93

**SUN HOUSE, M. Fry, 1935.** A house by Maxwell
Fry who in 1934-6 worked with Gropius, when
the German architect was in England for a few
years before moving to the United States. A
three-storeyed building with entrance and gar-
age on the right-hand side and projecting terrace, first floor balcony of the same length as the
façade, window band of different heights. «The
effect is surprising and shows what a design of
quality can make of relatively elementary material» (Pevsner). [Frognal Way, Hampstead].

a

b

c

d

## 94

**ROEHAMPTON, LCC, 1952-56.** The Roehampton estate, «probably the finest low-cost development in the world» (G.E. Kidder Smith), was designed by the architects J.L. Martin, R.H. Matthew and H. Bennett in 1952-56 for the London County Council. The estate is divided into two parts, Alton East, started first, and **Alton West**, the one here illustrated and undoubtedly the most successful. Based on the principal of combining high and low buildings, it accommodates about 10,000 people in some 2,611 dwellings (with a population density of 110 people to the acre) and it is formed by twelve-storey blocks and slab buildings, units of two-, three- and four-storey terraced houses and single storey houses for old people, a very original conception (illustration a, foreground). All the trees have been religiously left intact and they contribute to create a wonder-fully varied green landscape, with the differen levels of the ground happily exploited. The larg slab buildings are clearly derived from Le Corbu sier's Unités and they are sheathed, like the tow er blocks, with prefabricated concrete unit Less successful, from an architectural point c view, are the terraced houses, but what counts a Roehampton is the great visual variety of lands cape, particularly looking down towards Rich mond Park from Clarence Lane, the tall whit buildings rise majestically among the trees an give a new meaning to the idea of the housing es tate. Alton West also incorporates two distin guished XVIII c. buildings, Manresa House (5C and Mount Clare, a country house built probabl by Henry Holland in 1772 and now used as school.

**5**

**ЭUSFIELD SCHOOL, Chamberlin, Powell and ɔn, 1956.** One of the best schools since the war, ailt for the London County Council in 1956. In s field Britain's achievement is recognised all ⁀er the world, witness the Milan Triennale rand Prix of 1960 given to a prefabricated Brit- ำ school. This elementary school, also largely ᶒfabricated, is very discreetly inserted in its re- ᶁential neighbourhood by exploiting the differ- ᶇt ground levels, although it accommodates ᶈ0 pupils. Seen from the entrance, beyond the ᵃter garden which separates the school from ᵉ road, this building, surrounded by trees and ᵉen lawns, shows a very sensitive and delicate ᵈe of spaces and volumes recalling Japanese ᵃhitecture. [The Boltons, South Kensington].

**96**

**ROYAL COLLEGE OF ART, H.T. Cadbury-Brown, H. Casson and R. Goodden, 1962.** An impressive building, boldly designed, with its skyline of tall, square studio windows, it seems somehow to in- terpret in contemporary terms the traditional Tu- dor palace. It consists of three units, an eight- storey teaching-workshop block, overlooking the park, a four-storey common room and library block at the back; the two blocks are linked by the low hall and gallery wing on the E side. [Ken- sington Gore].

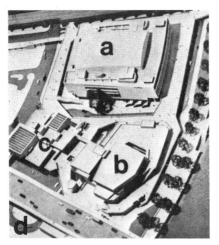

a - Royal Festival Hall
b - Queen Elizabeth Hall
c - Hayward Gallery
d - National Theatre

## 97

**THE SOUTH BANK ARTS CENTRE, LCC/GL**
**1951/1967-8.** The **Royal Festival Hall**, built f
the LCC by the architects R. Matthew and J.
Martin in 1951, is the first important example
modern architecture after the war (recently r
faced). The concert hall proper, for 3,000, is a s
parate body raised off the ground, enclosed w
thin the external structure and standing on r
tracted pillars. This independence of the tv
structures allows great freedom in the treatme
of space for the entrance halls, staircases, te
races, restaurants, etc., and this is certainly tl
most fascinating aspect of the building. Externa
ly the curved roof of the hall rises above the e
ternal walls, thus underlining the double stru
ture. In 1967 was opened the adjacent **Que**
**Elizabeth Hall** with two new concert halls, one f
1,106 and the other for 372 people. It was d
signed by the Architects Department of the GL
following the brutalistic trend then fashionabl
The flow of steps and terraces towards the riv
is spectacular. Of a similar architectural conce
tion is the **Hayward Gallery** at the back, designe
by Hubert Bennett for the GLC and opened
1968. With its four exhibition galleries it provid
a new important art centre for the capital. Thes
three modern buildings form thus a cultural cit
del to which the **National Theatre** was added o
the East side of Waterloo Bridge by Denis La
dun in 1976.

## 98

**ISMAILI CENTRE, Casson Conder Partnership, 1983.** The Ismaili Centre designed for the Ismaili Muslim community as a religious, cultural and social meeting point, was completed in 1983 by the Casson Conder Partnership. Erected on a prominent island site in South Kensington, opposite the Victoria and Albert Museum, it relates appropriately to the houses that lie to the South, it is a two storey building with a roof garden at the top. It is a most discreet and elegant design, once again a strange feeling pervades it (see no. 95), it has a certain Oriental refinement without mimicking any particular style. Islamic architecture is hinted at but never copied, it is certainly not classical in a historical sense, though it shows a somehow classical quality which goes very well with its Georgian London environment. A quality which is expressed by the lightness of the colour, the sparkling surface, the flat planes with only the most subtle modulation of decorative elements, always disciplined by geometry. All this is emphasized by graphic motifs which have been worked into the granite face of the building, whereas the interior design is enlivened by patterns of blue and white painted grooves and by gently vaulted ceilings (Council Chamber and Reading Room). A most inventive and surprising building, nicely controlled in all its aspects, qualities which remind us of the work of Sir John Soane, it has in fact that independence from styles which has always been typical of the British architectural tradition. It is one of the best buildings of the post war period in London. [Cromwell Road, South Kensington].

## 99

**CLORE GALLERY, TURNER MUSEUM, TATE GALLERY, James Stirling Michael Wilford and Associates, 1980-1985.** James Stirling designed this extension as a garden building with a separate but linked identity to the main building. The entrance of the new building avoids facing on to the river, thus eliminating any competition to the classical portico of the main block. The garden facades have panelling of stone with rendered infill (stucco). Service facades have by contrast light-coloured brickwork with coloured metal window elements. Galleries are on the upper level (at the same level as the Tate Gallery itself) giving uninterrupted circulation.

Non-exhibition spaces, lecture theatre, conservation department are below. The new gallery provides a superb display area for the historic collection of paintings and drawings by William Turner as well as much-needed ancillary facilities for the Tate Gallery. Recognised as Stirling and Wilford's mainstream post-modernist standpoint, this new building probably denied the architects the chance to build their excellent National Gallery extension scheme in Trafalgar Square, the commission ultimately being awarded to Venturi/Rauch/Scott Brown (1987). [Tate Gallery, Millbank, SWI].

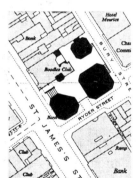

## 100

**ECONOMIST BUILDING, A. and P. Smithso**
**1964.** Three octagonal buildings groupe
around an open courtyard above street level.
should be noticed how the front building is di
creetly inserted in the townscape of St. James
Street, respecting particularly the scale of th
adjacent XVIII c. Boodles Club and preparing th
eye for the sight of the tower behind it. But th
most fascinating aspect of these buildings is th
new environment they create; a pedestrian pla
form with porticoes surrounded by streets at di
ferent levels, a space which is open and protec
ed at the same time, and which allows the su
rounding townscape to be enjoyed in a new ar
unexpected way. A lesson in civic design in th
best tradition of English town planning and
most appropriate conclusion, it seems to us, t
this selection of some of the most significant bu
dings in London.

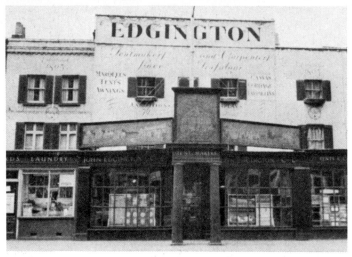

## 101

**SHOP SIGNS.** A Saxon tombstone; the stylized decoration of the Opus Anglicanum or an illuminated missal of the time; the rectangular «compartments» that are continually repeated in Tudor architecture; Robert Adam's neo-classical stuccoes; William Morris's cloths and wallpapers, or the precise, careful, lettering on the signs in the London underground, – all these illustrate a particular and extraordinary unchanging element in the English figurative arts. To be more specific, they show that marked preference for decorating surfaces geometrically that Roger Fry has called «a national mania for beautiful surface quality». This love of surface decoration, in painting and sculpture, in architecture and the applied arts, can well be defined – using another of Fry's expression – as «essentially linear», or, in other words, graphic.

Speaking of English architecture, Nikolaus Pevsner mentions a «national preference for the flat wall»; with this in mind, let us imagine the wall as a page. England, for example, completely, or almost completely refused both the baroque and the rococo. There are various historical and climatic reasons for this. The typical English light is soft and tenuous; when the sun makes its infre-

quent appearances through the clouds, it doe not shine with the fierce light that would bring o the highlights and deep shadows of baroque a chitecture. With so little light, large windows a necessary, like those we see in the countr houses of the Tudor period; in fact, these house have more glass than wall – and what materi can be flatter than glass? In the eighteenth cer tury, the use of these flat surfaces was brought such a point that some rows of small houses the period look extraordinary modern, in th manner of Gropius. The smooth, white, stuccoe façades offer an irresistible invitation to consid the walls as pages on which print is to be set o – and the English, in a certain sense, have dor just this.

Here we find graphic art of an ingenuous kin stemming from the people themselves, often wi an instinct for what is clean, tidy, and, at the sar time, decorative. Thus in residential quarters li Belgravia and Chelsea, we find numbers of sm houses whose doors are painted in brilliant cc lours, each one different from its neighbou Moreover, in Belgravia especially, this custo fits in perfectly with the architecture in a quart that was designed and built at the most «theatr

al» moment of the Regency period, when archi-cture became a question of a purely scenic in-rplay, and the buildings themselves no more an play-things.

he little shopkeeper in the East End, on the :her hand, makes use of his lovely white wall as kind of «house magazine», offering the public s goods or his services as if he were creating e layout of an advertisement in a newspaper.

f course, the English graphic genius is also to e seen in the work done by professionals. It is a ell-known fact that some of the classic modern pefaces were designed by English typograph-rs, such as John Baskerville, Eric Gill or Stanley 'orrison; it was the latter who especially created e beautiful «Times» characters, for the most im-ortant of the English newspapers.

'ith such a history behind them, the shop signs ill always be clear and easily-read, the books rinted on good paper and strongly-bound, the gnboards carefully painted and decorated; this true whether one is speaking of an eighteenth-entury shop, or a Art-Nouveau-style pub, or the dicator-signs in the underground stations or at e bus stops. As a matter of interest, the London ansport signs, with their strong, clear Gill cha-

racters, have been in use since 1930. In fact, London transport was probably the first of the world's great organizations to adopt its own «house style» as a part of company policy.

This rigorousness in the graphic arts must be seen in relation to the strength of the classical and neo-classical traditions in England. Yet classicism and romanticism are two permanent, though opposing elements in English culture, one might say, in the English mind. Take, for example, the «theatrical» architecture of the Regency period (the structural «nonsense» of the John Nash terraces); the parts that go to make up the whole are perfectly classical in style. This marriage of fantasy and precision helps to explain the door of different colours which we mentioned earlier, as well as the strangeness of certain signboards to be seen in every part of the country, or the unexpectedness of a number of very small, but extremely elaborate Victorian constructions, which seem to parody every known style and are no more than architectural toys, made purely for amusement and not without a touch of humour, which is, in itself, very English.

**London shops.** Several London shops still preserve original shop fronts and interiors, some dating from the late eighteenth century, if not earlier. They are mostly to be found in the old «villages» of London, Hampstead, Fulham, Richmond, Greenwich, etc., and hark back to past centuries, intimate, well-lit (large windows), a bit strange to see in a modern city, this is old England, like entering the world of Beatrix Potter or of «Alice in Wonderland». To introduce this world of yesterday some shop signs are illustrated here, ranging from strict Georgian to elaborate Victorian styles with a hint of Art Nouveau (some of these signs may have disappeared in the meantime, but similar ones will be easily found in the London streets). They represent a considerable variety of types, going from aristocratic shops selling antique silver, umbrellas, or made-to-measure shoes or hats, to more popular grocer's shops, undertakers premises, tobacconists or pubs. They are very different signs but they all have in common a certain elegance in their lettering and a clarity of layout, that is to say a graphic quality which makes them unmistakeably British.

H.P. Berlage, Holland House, 1914; (b) B. Lubetkin, Penguin Pool in the London Zoo, 1934-38; (c) W. Crabtree/C. Reilly, Peter Jones Department Store, 1936.

## FURTHER SELECTION OF BUILDINGS

Buildings marked thus (*) are of particular interest.

### Roman remains

St. Albans (Verulamium), Hertfordshire.

### Norman

- St. John, Clerkenwell, crypt, 1140-85.
  St. Albans Cathedral, Hertfordshire, from 1077.
- Waltham Abbey, Essex, late XII c.

### Gothic

St. Helen Bishopsgate, 1314-17.
- St. Etheldreda, Ely Place, Holborn, c. 1300.
- St. Stephen, Westminster, crypt, 1319-27.
  Penshurst Place, Kent, 1341.
- Eltham Palace, Kent, XII-XV c.

### Late Gothic

Crosby Hall, Chelsea, 1470.
St. Margaret, Westminster, 1504-23.
St. Dunstan, Stepney, late XV c.
- St. Giles, Cripplegate, 1545.
St. George's Chapel, Windsor, late XV c.
Eton College, Chapel and Quadrangle, 1441-8.
- Guildhall, crypt, XV c.
* Lambeth Palace, XV-XVI c.
* Old Buildings, Lincoln's Inn, XVI c.
- Staple Inn, Holborn, 1585.
- Fulham Palace, early XVI c.
- St. Peter ad Vincula, Tower of London, early XVI c.
* Sutton Place, Surrey, 1523.

### XVII century

- Inner Temple Gateway, Strand, 1610.
- St. Katharine Cree, 1628-31.
- Ham House, 1636-73.
* Presbytery, Croom's Hill, Greenwich, 1630.
* Hatfield House, Hertfordshire, 1607-11.
* Knole House, Kent, early XVII c.
* Audley End, Essex, 1603-16.
* Lincoln's Inn, New Square, 1690.
* Fenton House, Hampstead, 1693.

Wren:
- The Monument, 1671-77.
* Greenwich Observatory, 1675.
- Marlborough House, 1709-10.
* St. Mary-at-Hill, 1670-6.
- St. James Garlickhythe, 1674-87.
* St. Magnus, London Bridge, 1676.
* St. Benet Paul's Wharf, 1677-85.
* St. Martin Ludgate, 1677-87.
- St. Peter Cornhill, 1677-87.
- St. Bride Fleet Street, 1680.
* St. Mary Abchurch, 1681-6.
- St. Michael Paternoster Royal, 1686-94.
- St. Margaret Lothbury, 1686-1701.
- Christ Church, Newgate Street, steeple, 1704.

### XVIII century

* Spanish and Portuguese Synagogue, Bevis Marks, 1700.
- Blue Coat School, Westminster, 1702.
- Vanbrugh Castle, Greenwich, J. Vanbrugh, 1717.

(a) P. Moro, Hille Building, 1962; (b) D. Lasdun, Royal College of Physicians, 1964; (c) E. Saarinen, USA Embassy, 1962.

* St. George Bloomsbury, N. Hawksmoor, 1720-31.
* Burlington House, C. Campbell, 1715.
* Mereworth Castle, C. Campbell, 1722.
- St. George, Hanover Square, J. James, 1713-24.
- St. Peter, Vere Street, J. Gibbs, 1721-24.
* Moor Park, Hertfordshire, G. Leoni, 1720.
- Argyll House, Chelsea, G. Leoni, 1723.
- St. Luke, Old Street, G. Dance the Elder, 1732-3.
- St. Leonard, Shoreditch, G. Dance the Elder, 1736-40.
- Admiralty Screen, R. Adam, 1759.
- Asgill House, Richmond, R. Taylor, 1765.
- Albany, W. Chambers, 1770.
- Ely House, Dover Street, R. Taylor, 1772.
* Stone Buildings, Lincoln's Inn, R. Taylor, 1774.
- 46-8 Portland Place, J. Adam, 1774.
- Boodle's Club, J. Crunden, 1775.
* Brooks Club, H. Holland, 1777-8.
- Bedford Square, T. Leverton, 1775.
- St. Mary, Paddington Green, J. Plaw, 1788-91.
- Trinity House, Trinity Square, S. Wyatt, 1792-4.
* XVIII century houses:
    Chelsea, Cheyne Walk.
    Highgate, The Green.
    Richmond, The Green.

## XIX century

* Pitzhanger Manor, Ealing, J. Soane, 1801-2.
- Royal Artillery Barracks, Woolwich, completed 1802.
- St. Anne, Soho, steeple, S.P. Cockerell, 1806.
- Rotunda, Woolwich, J. Nash, 1814-19.
* St. Pancras Church, N.W. Inwood, 1819-22.
- Greenwich Market, J. Kay, 1831.
* Travellers' and Reform Clubs, C. Barry, 1829-41.
- British Museum, S. Smirke, 1823.
- Athenaeum Club, D. Burton, 1829.
- The Record Office, J. Pennerthone, 1857-66.
* Palace Green, Kensington, P. Webb, 1863.

- Foreign Office, G.G. Scott, 1868-73.
* Law Courts, G. Street, 1868-92.
- St. Augustine, Kilburn, J.L. Pearson, 1879.
- Leadenhall Market, City, H. Jones, 1881.
* Lululand, Melbourne Road, Bushey, H.H. Richardson, 1885.
- Holy Trinity, Latimer Street, N. Shaw, 1887-
- Holy Trinity, Sloane Square, S. Seeding, Moris & Co., 1888-90.
- Scotland Yard, N. Shaw, 1888.
- Westminster Cathedral, J. Bentley, 1895-1903.
* 37-39 Cheyne Walk, C.E. Ashbee, 1894-190-
* Annesley Lodge, Hampstead, C.F. Voyse 1895.
* Maryward Settlement, Tavistock Place, Smit & Brewer, 1897.

## XX century

* The Orchard and Hollybank, Shire Lane Chorleywood, C.F. Voysey, 1900-4.
* Hampstead Garden Suburb, B. Parker & R. Urwin, 1906.
- Rhodesia House, Strand, C. Holden, 1907.
* Holland House, Bury Lane, EC, H.B. Berlage 1914.
- Battersea Power Station, G. Scott, 1928.
* Arnos Grove Underground Station, C. Holder 1932.
* Penguin Pool, Zoo, Tecton Group, 1934-8.
- Simpson's Piccadilly, J. Emberton, 1935.
* Peter Jones Dept Store, Sloane Square, S.W W. Crabtree/C. Reilly, 1936.
* 66 Old Church Street, Chelsea, W. Gropius 1936.
- Churchill Gardens, Powell & Moya, from 1947
- Golden Lane Estate, Chamberlin, Powell & Bon, 1953-64.
- Cluster Block, Bethnal Green, D. Lasdur 1956-60.
* Langham House Close, Ham Common, Stirling & Gowan, 1958.
* Youth Hostel, Holland Park, H. Casson, 1959

R. Rogers, Lloyd's Building, 1978-86; (b) CZWG Architects, Cascades, Housing on the Isle of Dogs, London Docklands, 1988; (c) nturi/Rauch/Scott Brown, Sainsbury Wing, National Gallery, 1986-89.

Castrol House, Gollins, Melvin, Ward, 1959.
Peter Robinson, Strand, D. Lasdun, 1959.
Holland Park School, L. Martin, 1959.
USA Embassy, Grosvenor Square, W1, E. Saarinen, 1962.
Hille Building, Mayfair, P. Moro, 1962.
Eros House, Catford, O. Luder, 1962.
Barbican, Chamberlin, Powell & Bon, from 1963.
Brunswick Park School, Camberwell, J. Stirling & J. Gowan, 1963.
Royal College of Physicians, Regent's Park, D. Lasdun, 1964.
Civic Centre, Swiss Cottage, B. Spence, 1965.
Zoo Pavilions, H. Casson, 1965.
Choir School, St. Paul's Cathedral, Architects' Co-Partnership, 1967.
Jack Straw's Castle, North End Way, Hampstead, NW3, Raymond Erith and Quinlan Terry, 1964.
125 Park Road, NW8, Farrell/Grimshaw Partnership, 1970.
Pimlico Comprehensive School, SW1, GLC Department of Architecture and Civic Design, 1970.
− Centre Point, St Giles Circus, WC1, R Seifert & Partners, 1971.
− The Young Vic, 66 The Cut, SE1, Howell, Killick, Partridge and Amis, 1971.
* Robin Hood Gardens, Poplar, E, Alison and Peter Smithson, 1972.
− Brunswick Centre, Brunswick Square, WC1, Patrick Hodgkinson, 1973.
− Chelsea Football Club, East Stand, Stamford Bridge, Fulham Road, SW6, Darbourne and Dark, 1973.
* Warehouse and Showroom for Modern Art Glass Ltd, Hailey Road, Thamesmead, Foster Associates, 1973.
− 36-38 Leadenhall Street, EC3, Yorke Rosenberg Mardall, 1973.
− Children's Reception Home, Alexandra Road, Camden, Eldred Evans and David Shalev, 1976.
− British Library, Euston Road, NW1, Colin St John Wilson & Partners, 1990.

# Acknowledgements

Front cover: Lloyd's Building: Architectural Association / Valerie Bennett.

*Architectural Association, London:* page 113 (a), Marjorie Morrison, page 113 (b) Valerie Bennett, page 115 (a/b) Valerie Bennett, no. 49 E.R. Jarret, no. 84 C. Parsons, no. 98 Valerie Bennett, no. 97 Jane Beckett.

*British Travel Association:* page, 2, 8, no. 3 (a/b), 6 (a/f), 9, 12, 13, 14, 21 (c), 22, 24 (a-c), 29, 32 (a/c), 33 (a/b), 34 (b), 45, 51, 58 (a/b), 60, 62, 69 (a/b), 74, 76, 79 (a/b), 82, 83, 91, 93 97.

*Romano Cagnoni:* no. 19, 21 (b), 27, 28, 35, 42, 43, 44, 46 (a-c), 53, 61 (a), 63, 66 (a/b), 71 (a-c-d-h), 73, 72, 75, 81 (a/b), 85 (a), 87, 88, 89, 93, 101.

*Central Office of Information, Crown Copyright:* no. 7, 18, 24 (b), 46 (b), 55, 61 (b), 65, 77 (b), 94 (c).

*The Economist:* no. 100 (a/b).

*Greater London Council,* reproduced by permission of Hubert Bennett, F.R.I.B.A., F.S.I.A., Architect to the G.L.C.: no. 26, 38, 40, 48 (a/b).

*A.F. Kersting:* no. 25, 37, 41, 70, 71 (e).

*Frank Monaco:* no. 10 (b), 17, 21, 39 (a/b), 47, 71 (m/n), 99.

*National Monuments Record, Crown Copyright:* no. 8, 54, 56, 57, 59, 67, 68, 85 (b).

*Royal Commission on Historical Monuments (England):* no. 21 (a).

*Antonio Salvadori:* no. 1, 2, 4, 5 (a/b), 10 (a), 11 (a/b), 15, 16, 20, 23, 30, 34 (a-c), 36, 49, 50, 52 (a/c), 64, 71 (b-g-i-l), 77 (a), 78, 80 (a/c), 86, 90, 94 (a/d), 95, 96 (a/b).

*Peter Wyld,* drawings on pages 12, 16, 17, 66.